Prayer And Praying Men

Edward M. Bounds

DESTINY IMAGE® PUBLISHERS, INC.
P.O. Box 310, Shippensburg, PA 17257-0310

"*Speaking to the Purposes of God for this Generation and for the
Generations to Come.*"

This book and all other Destiny Image, Revival Press, Mercy Place,
Fresh Bread, Destiny Image Fiction, and Treasure House books are
available at Christian bookstores and distributors worldwide.

For a U.S. bookstore nearest you, call 1-800-722-6774.

For more information on foreign distributors, call 717-532-3040.

Or reach us on the Internet: www.destinyimage.com.z

ISBN 10: 0-7684-2546-8
ISBN 13: 978-0-7684-2546-8

For Worldwide Distribution, Printed in the U.S.A.

1 2 3 4 5 6 7 8 9 10 / 10 09 08 07

Contents

Introduction 5

Chapter 1
Praying Saints of the Old Testament 11

Chapter 2
Praying Saints of the Old Testament (continued) 21

Chapter 3
Abraham, The Man of Prayer .31

Chapter 4
Moses, The Mighty Intercessor 37

Chapter 5
Elijah, The Praying Prophet 49

Chapter 6
Hezekiah, The Praying King 63

Chapter 7
Ezra, The Praying Reformer 77

Chapter 8
Nehemiah, The Praying Builder .85

Chapter 9
Samuel, The Child of Prayer 95

Chapter 10
Daniel, The Praying Captive 105

Chapter 11
Faith of Sinners in Prayer 115

Chapter 12
Paul, The Teacher of Prayer 127

Chapter 13
Paul and His Praying 143

Chapter 14
Paul and His Praying (continued) 155

Chapter 15
Paul and His Requests for Prayer 169

Chapter 16
Paul and His Requests for Prayer (continued) 179

Introduction

Rev. Edward McKendrie Bounds was passionately devoted to his beloved Lord and Saviour Jesus Christ. His devotion was extraordinary in that he was praying and writing about Him all the time, except during the hours of sleeping.

God gave Bounds an enlargedness of heart and an insatiable desire to do service for Him. To this end he enjoyed what I am pleased to term a transcendent inspiration, else he could never have brought out of his treasury things new and old far exceeding anything we have known or read in the last half century.

Bounds is easily the Betelguese of the devotional sky. There is no man that has lived since the days of the apostles that has surpassed him in the depths of his marvelous research into the Life of Prayer.

He was busily engaged in writing on his manuscripts when the Lord said unto him, "Well done, thou good and faithful servant, enter thou into the joys of thy Lord." His letters would often come to me in Brooklyn, N.Y., in 1911, 1912 and 1913, saying, "Pray for me that God will give me new nerves and new visions to finish the manuscripts."

Wesley was of the sweetest and most forgiving disposition, but when aroused he was a man of the "keenest penetration with a gift of speech that bit like the stroke of a whip." Bounds was meek and humble, and never did we know him to retaliate upon any of his enemies. He cried over them and wept praying for them early and late.

Wesley was easily gulled. "My brother," said Charles, on one occasion in disgusting accents, "was, I believe, born for the benefit of knaves." No man could impose on Bounds' credulity. He was a diagnostician of rare ability. Bounds shied away from all frauds in profession, and would waste no time upon them.

Wesley was preaching and riding all day. Bounds was praying and writing day and night.

Wesley would not allow any misrepresentation of his doctrinal positions in his late years. Bounds in this respect was very much like him.

Wesley came to his fame while yet alive. He was always in the public eye. Bounds, while editing a Christian Advocate for twelve years, was little known out of his church.

Wesley at eighty-six could still preach on the streets for thirty minutes. Bounds was able at seventy-five in the first hour of the fourth watch to pray for three hours upon his knees.

Wesley, at the time of his death had enjoyed fifty-six years of preferment. His name was on every tongue. Christianity was born again in England under his mighty preaching and organization. Bounds was comparatively unknown for fifty years but will recover the "lost and forgotten secret of the Church" in the next fifty years.

Wesley's piety and genius and popularity flowed from his early life like a majestic river. Bounds has been dammed up, but now it is beginning to sweep with resistless force and ere long he will be the mighty Amazon of the devotional world.

Henry Crabbe Robinson said in his diary when he heard Wesley preach at Colchester, "He stood in a wide pulpit and on each side of him stood a minister, and the two held him up. His voice was feeble and he could hardly be heard, but his reverend countenance, especially his long white locks, formed a picture never to be forgotten." The writer of these lines gave up his pulpit in Brooklyn in 1912 to Rev. E. M. Bounds just ten months before his death. His voice was feeble and his periods were not rounded out. His sermon was only twenty minutes long, when he quietly came to the end and seemed exhausted.

Wesley had sufficient money and to spare during all his career. Bounds did not care for money. He did not depreciate it; he considered it the lowest order of power.

Wesley died with "an eye beaming and lips breaking into praise." "The best of all is God with us," Bounds wrote the writer of these lines. "When He is ready I am ready; I long to taste the joys of the heavenlies."

Wesley said, "The World is my parish." Bounds prayed as if the universe was his zone.

Wesley was the incarnation of unworldliness, the embodiment of magnanimity. Bounds was the incarnation of unearthliness, humility and self-denial. Wesley will live in the hearts of saints for everlasting ages. Bounds eternally.

Wesley sleeps in City Road Chapel grounds, among his "bonny dead," under marble, with fitting tribute chiseled in prose, awaiting the Resurrection. Bounds sleeps in Washington, Georgia, cemetery, without marble covering, awaiting the Bridegroom's coming.

These two men held ideals high and dear beyond the reach of other men. Has this race of men entirely gone out of the world now that they are dead? Let us pray.

Homer W. Hodge

Brooklyn, N.Y.

Chapter 1

Praying Saints of the Old Testament

The Holy Spirit will give to the praying saint the brightness of an immortal hope, the music of a deathless song, in His baptism and communion with the heart, He will give sweeter and more enlarged visions of Heaven until the taste for other things will pall, and other visions will grow dim and distant. He will put notes of other worlds in human hearts until all earth's music is discord and songless.

—Rev. E. M. Bounds

Old Testament history is filled with accounts of praying saints. The leaders of Israel in those early days were noted for their praying habits. Prayer is the one thing which stands out prominently in their lives.

To begin with, note the incident in Joshua 10, where the very heavenly bodies were made subject to prayer. A prolonged battle was on between the Israelites and their enemies, and when night was rapidly coming on, and it was discovered that a few more hours of daylight were needful to ensure victory for the Lord's hosts, Joshua, that sturdy man of God, stepped into the breach, with prayer. The sun was too rapidly declining in the west for God's people to reap the full fruits of a noted victory, and Joshua, seeing how much depended upon

Application to My Life:

the occasion, cried out in the sight and in the hearing of Israel, "Sun, stand thou still upon Gideon, and thou moon in the Valley of Ajalon." And the sun actually stood still and the moon stopped on her course at the command of this praying man of God, till the Lord's people had avenged themselves upon the Lord's enemies.

Jacob was not a strict pattern of righteousness, prior to his all-night praying. Yet he was a man of prayer and believed in the God of prayer. So we find him swift to call upon God in prayer when he was in trouble. He was fleeing from home fearing Esau, on his way to the home of Laban, a kinsman. As night came on, he lighted on a certain place to refresh himself with sleep, and as he slept he had a wonderful dream in which he saw the angels of God ascending and descending on a ladder which stretched from earth to heaven. It was no wonder when he awoke he was constrained to exclaim, "Surely the Lord is in this place and I knew it not."

Then it was he entered into a very definite covenant with Almighty God, and in prayer vowed a vow unto the Lord, saying, "If God will be with me, and will keep me in this way that I go, and will give me bread to eat and raiment to put on, so that I come again to my father's house in peace; and shall the Lord be my God, and this stone which I have set for a pillar shall be God's house; and of all that thou shalt give me, I will surely give one-tenth unto thee."

With a deep sense of his utter dependence upon God, and desiring above all the help of God, Jacob conditioned his prayer for protection, blessing and guidance by a solemn vow. Thus Jacob supported his prayer to God by a vow.

Twenty years had passed while Jacob tarried at the house of Laban, and he had married two of his daughters and God had given him children. He had increased largely in wealth, and he resolved to leave that place and return home to where he had been reared. Nearing home it occurred to him that he must meet his brother Esau, whose anger had not abated notwithstanding the passage of many years. God, however, had said to him, "Return to thy father's house and to thy kindred, and I will be with thee." In this dire emergency doubtless God's promise and His vow made long ago came to his mind, and he took himself to an all-night season of prayer. Here comes to our notice that strange, inexplicable incident of the angel struggling with Jacob all night long, till Jacob at last obtained the victory. "I will not let thee go except thou bless me." And then and there, in answer to his earnest, pressing and importunate praying, he was richly blessed personally and his name was changed. But even more than that, God went ahead of Jacob's desire, and strangely moved upon the angry nature

Application to My Life:

of Esau, and lo and behold, when Jacob met him next day, Esau's anger had entirely abated, and he vied with Jacob in showing kindness to his brother who had wronged him. No explanation of this remarkable change in the heart of Esau is satisfactory which leaves out prayer.

Samuel, the mighty intercessor in Israel and a man of God, was the product of his mother's prayer. Hannah is a memorable example of the nature and benefits of importunate praying. No son had been born to her and she yearned for a man child. Her whole soul was in her desire. So she went to the house of worship, where Eli, the priest of God, was, and staggering under the weight of which bore down on her heart she was beside herself and seemed to be really intoxicated. Her desires were too intense for articulation. "She poured out her soul in prayer before the Lord." Insuperable natural difficulties were in the way, but she "multiplied her praying," as the passage means, till her God-lightened heart and her bright face recorded the answer to her prayers, and Samuel was hers by a conscious faith and a nation was restored by faith.

Samuel was born in answer to the vowful prayer of Hannah, for the solemn covenant which she made with God if He would grant her request must not be left out of the account in investigating this incident of a praying woman and the answer she received. It is suggestive in James 5:15 that "The prayer of faith shall save the sick," the word translated means a vow. So that prayer in its highest form of faith is that prayer which carries the whole man as a sacrificial offering. Thus devoting the whole man himself, and his all, to God in a definite, intelligent vow, never to be broken, in a quenchless and impassioned desire for heaven—such an attitude of self-devotement to God mightily helps praying. Samson is somewhat of a paradox when we examine his religious character. But amid all his faults, which were grave in the extreme, he knew the God who hears prayer and he knew how to talk to God.

No farness to which Israel had gone, no depth to which Israel had fallen, no chains however iron with which Israel was bound but that their cry to God easily spanned the distance, fathomed the depths, and broke the chains. It was the lesson they were ever learning and always forgetting, that prayer always brought God to their deliverance, and that there was nothing too hard for God to do for His people. We find all of God's saints in straits at different times in some way or another. Their straits are, however, often the heralds of their great triumphs. But for whatever cause their straits come, or of what kind soever, there is no strait of any degree of direness or from any source whatsoever of any nature whatsoever, from which prayer could not extricate them. The great strength of Samson does

Application to My Life:

not relieve him nor extricate him out of his straits. Read what the Scriptures say:

"And when he came unto Lehi, the Philistines shouted against him; and the Spirit of the Lord came mightily upon him, and the cords that were upon his arms became as flax that was burnt with fire, and his bands loosed from off his hands.

"And he found a new jawbone of an ass, and put forth his hand, and took it, and slew a thousand men therewith.

"And Samson said, With the jawbone of an ass, heaps upon heaps, with the jawbone of an ass have I slain a thousand men.

"And it came to pass when he had made an end of speaking, that he cast away the jawbone out of his hand, and called that place Ramath-Lehi.

"And he was sore athirst, and called on the Lord, and said, Thou hast given this great deliverance into the hand of thy servant, and now shall I die of thirst, and fall into the hand of the uncircumcised?

"But God clave a hollow place that was in the jaw, and there came water thereout; and when he had drunk, his spirit came again and he revived."

We have another incident in the case of this strange Old Testament character, showing how, when in great straits, their minds involuntarily turned to God in prayer. However irregular in life they were, however far from God they departed, however sinful they might be when trouble came upon these men, they invariably called upon God for deliverance, and, as a rule, when they repented God heard their cries and granted their requests. This incident comes at the close of Samson's life, and shows us how his life ended.

Read the record as found in Judges 16. Samson had formed an alliance with Delilah, a heathen woman, and she, in connivance with the Philistines, sought to discover the source of his immense strength. Three successive times she failed, and at last by her persistence and womanly arts persuaded Samson to divulge to her the wonderful secret. So in an unsuspecting hour he disclosed to her the fact that the source of his strength was in his hair which had never been cut; and she deprived him of his great physical power by cutting off his hair. She called for the Philistines, and they came and put out his eyes and otherwise mistreated him.

On an occasion when the Philistines were gathered together to offer a great sacrifice to Dagon, their idol god, they called for Samson to make sport for them. And the following is the account as he stood there presumably the laughing-stock of these enemies of his and of God.

Application to My Life:

"And Samson said unto the lad that held him by the hand, Suffer me that I may feel the pillars whereupon the house standeth, that I may lean upon them.

"Now the house was full of men and women; and all the lords of the Philistines were there; and there were upon the roof about three thousand men and women, that beheld while Samson made sport.

"And Samson called unto the Lord and said, O Lord God, remember me, I pray thee, and strengthen me, I pray thee, only this once, my God, that I may be at once avenged of the Philistines for my two eyes. And Samson took hold of the two middle pillars upon which the house stood, and on which it was borne up, of the one with his right hand and of the other with his left.

"And Samson said, Let me die with the Philistines. And he bowed himself with all his might, and the house fell upon the lords, and upon all the people that were there within. So the dead which he slew at his death were more than they which he slew in his life."

Chapter 2

Praying Saints of the Old Testament (Continued)

Bishop Lambeth and Wainwright had a great M. E. Mission in Osaka, Japan. One day the order came from high up that no more meetings would be allowed in the city by Protestants. Lambeth and Wainwright did all they could but the high officials were obstinate and unrelenting. They then retired to the room of prayer. Supper time came and the Japanese girl came to summon them to their meal, but she fell under the power of prayer. Mrs. Lambeth came to find what the matter was and fell under the same power. They then rose and went to the mission hall and opened it: and at once commenced meeting. God fell upon the assembly and two of the sons of the city officials came to the altar and were saved. Next morning one of the officials in authority came to the mission and said, "Go on with your meetings, you will not be interrupted." The Osaka daily paper came out with box car letters saying, "THE CHRISTIAN'S GOD CAME TO TOWN LAST NIGHT."

—Rev. H. C. Morrison

Jonah, the man who prayed in the fish's belly, brings to view another remarkable instance of these Old Testament worthies who were given to prayer. This man Jonah, a prophet of the Lord, was a fugitive from God and from the place of duty. He had been sent on a mission of warning to wicked Nineveh, and had been commanded to cry out against them, "for their wickedness is come up before Me," said God. But Jonah, through fear or otherwise, declined to obey God, and took passage on a ship for Tarshish, fleeing from God. He seems to have overlooked the plain fact that the same God who had sent him on that alarming mission had His eye upon him as he hid himself on board that vessel. A storm arose as the vessel was on its way to Tarshish, and it was decided to throw Jonah overboard

Application to My Life:

in order to appease God and to avert the destruction of the boat and of all on board. But God was there as He had been with Jonah from the beginning. He had prepared a great fish to swallow Jonah, in order to arrest him, to defeat him in his flight from the post of duty, and to save Jonah that he might help to carry out the purposes of God.

It was Jonah who was in the fish's belly, in that great strait, and passing through a strange experience, who called upon God, who heard him and caused the fish to vomit him out on dry land. What possible force could rescue him from this fearful place? He seemed hopelessly lost, in "the belly of hell," as good as dead and damned. But he prays—what else can he do? And this is just what he had been accustomed to do when in trouble before.

"I cried by reason of my affliction unto the Lord, and he heard me; out of the belly of hell cried I, and thou heardst my voice."

And the Lord spake unto the fish, and it vomited out Jonah upon the dry land.

Like others he joined prayer to a vow he had made, for he says in his prayer, "But I will sacrifice unto thee with the voice of thanksgiving; I will pay that that I have vowed. Salvation is of the Lord."

Prayer was the mighty force which brought Jonah from "the belly of hell." Prayer, mighty prayer, has secured the end. Prayer brought God to the rescue of unfaithful Jonah, despite his sin of fleeing from duty, and God could not deny his prayer. Nothing is too hard for prayer because nothing is too hard for God.

That answered prayer of Jonah in the fish's belly in its mighty results became an Old Testament type of the miraculous power displayed in the resurrection of Jesus Christ from the dead. Our Lord puts His seal of truth upon the fact of Jonah's prayer and resurrection.

Nothing can be simpler than these cases of God's mighty deliverance. Nothing is plainer than that prayer has to do with God directly and simply. Nothing is clearer than that prayer has its only worth and significance in the great fact that God hears and answers prayer. This the Old Testament saints strongly believed. It is the one fact that stands out continuously and prominently in their lives. They were essentially men of prayer.

How greatly we need a school to teach the art of praying! This simplest of all arts and mightiest of all forces is ever in danger of being forgotten or depraved. The further we get away

Application to My Life:

from our mother's knees, the further do we get away from the true art of praying. All our after-schooling and our after-teachers unteach us the lessons of prayer. Men prayed well in Old Testament times because they were simple men and lived in simple times. They were childlike, lived in childlike times and had childlike faith.

In citing the Old Testament saints noted for their praying habits, by no means must David be overlooked, a man who preeminently was a man of prayer. With him prayer was a habit, for we hear him say, "Evening and morning and at noon will I pray and cry aloud." Prayer with the Sweet Psalmist of Israel was no strange occupation. He knew the way to God and was often found in that way. It is no wonder we hear his call so dear and impressive, "O come, let us worship and bow down; let us kneel before the Lord our Maker." He knew God as the one being who could answer prayer: "O thou that hearest prayer, to thee shall all flesh come."

When God smote the child born of Bathsheba, because David had by his grievous sins given occasion of the enemies of God to blaspheme, it is no surprise that we find him engaged in a week's prayer, asking God for the life of the child. The habit of his life asserted itself in this great emergency in his home, and we find him fasting and praying for the child to recover. The fact that God denied his request does not at all affect the question of David's habit of praying. Even though he did not receive what he asked for, his faith in God was not in the least affected. The fact is that while God did not give him the life of that baby boy, He afterward gave him another son, even Solomon. So that possibly the latter son was a far greater blessing to him than would have been the child for whom he prayed.

In close connection with this season of prayer, we must not overlook David's penitential praying when Nathan, by command of God, uncovered David's two great sins of adultery and murder. At once David acknowledged his wickedness, saying unto Nathan, "I have sinned." And as showing his deep grief over his sin, his heart-broken spirit, and his genuine repentance, it is only necessary to read Psalm 51 where confession of sin, deep humiliation and prayer are the chief ingredients of the Psalm.

David knew where to find a sin-pardoning God, and was received back again and had the joys of salvation restored to him by earnest, sincere, penitential praying. Thus are all sinners brought into the divine favor, thus do they find pardon, and thus do they find a new heart.

The entire Book of Psalms brings prayer to the front, and prayer fairly bristles before our eyes as we read this devotional book of the Scriptures.

Application to My Life:

Nor must even Solomon be overlooked in the famous catalogue of men who prayed in Old Testament times. Whatever their faults, they did not forget the God who hears prayer nor did they cease to seek the God of prayer. While this wise man in his later life departed from God, and his sun set under a cloud, we find him praying at the commencement of his reign.

Solomon went to Gibeon to offer sacrifice, which always meant that prayer went in close companionship with sacrifice, and while there, the Lord appeared to Solomon in a vision by night, saying unto him, "Ask what I shall give thee." The sequel shows the material out of which Solomon's character was formed. What was his request?

"O Lord my God, thou hast made thy servant king instead of my father; and I am but a little child; I know not how to go out or to come in.

"And thy servant is in the midst of thy people which thou hast chosen, a great people, that cannot be numbered nor counted for multitude.

"Give therefore thy servant an understanding heart to judge thy people, that I may discern between good and bad; for who is able to judge this thy so great a people?"

We do not wonder that it is recorded as a result of such praying:

"And the speech pleased the Lord, that Solomon had asked this thing.

"And God said unto him, Because thou hast asked this thing, and hast not asked for thyself long life; neither hast asked riches for thyself, nor hast asked the life of thy enemies, but has asked for thyself understanding to discern judgment;

"Behold I have done according to thy word; Lo, I have given thee a wise and understanding heart; so that there was none like thee before thee, neither after thee shall any arise like unto thee.

"Also I have given thee that which thou hast not asked, both riches and honor; so that there shall not be any among the kings like unto thee all thy days."

What praying was this! What self-deprecation and simplicity! "I am but a little child." How he specified the one thing needful! And see how much more he received than that for which he asked!

Take the remarkable prayer at the dedication of the temple. Possibly this is the longest recorded prayer in God's Word. How comprehensive, pointed, intensive, it is! Solomon could not afford to lay the foundations of God's house in anything

Application to My Life:

else but in prayer. And God heard this prayer as he heard him before, "And when Solomon had made an end of his praying, the fire came down from Heaven, and the glory of the Lord filled the house," thus God attested the acceptance of this house of worship and of Solomon, the praying king.

The list of these Old Testament saints given to prayer grows as we proceed, and is too long to notice at length all of them. But the name of Isaiah, the great evangelical prophet, and that of Jeremiah, the weeping prophet, must not be left out of the account. Still others might be mentioned. These are sufficient, and with their names we may close the list. Let careful readers of the Old Scriptures keep the prayer question in mind, and they will see how great a place prayer occupied in the minds and lives of the men of those early days.

Chapter 3

Abraham, The Man of Prayer

Oh for determined men and women, who will rise early and really burn out for God. Oh for a faith that will sweep into heaven with the early dawning of the morning and have ships from a shoreless sea loaded in the soul's harbor ere the ordinary laborer has knocked the dew from his scythe or the huckster has turned from his pallet of straw to spread nature's treasures of fruit before the early buyers.

—Rev. Homer W. Hodge

Abraham, the friend of God, was a striking illustration of one of the Old Testament saints who believed strongly in prayer. Abraham was not a shadowy figure by any means. In the simplicity and dimness of the patriarchal dispensation, as illustrated by him, we learn the worth of prayer, as well as discover its antiquity. The fact is, prayer reaches back to the first ages of man on earth. We see how the energy of prayer is absolutely required in the simplest as well as in the most complex dispensations of God's grace. When we study Abraham's character, we find that after his call to go out into an unknown country, on his journey with his family and his household servants, wherever he tarried by the way for the night or longer, he always erected an altar, and "called upon the name of the Lord." And this man of faith and prayer was one of the first to erect a family altar, around which to gather his household and offer the sacrifices of worship, of praise and of prayer. These altars built by Abraham were,

Application to My Life:

first of all, essentially altars about which he gathered his household, as distinguished from secret prayer.

As God's revelations became fuller and more perfect, Abraham's prayerfulness increased, and it was at one of these spiritual eras that "Abraham fell on his face and God talked with him." On still another occasion we find this man, "the father of the faithful," on his face before God, astonished almost to incredulity at the purposes and revelations of Almighty God to him in promising him a son in his old age, and the wonderful engagements which God made concerning his promised son.

Even Ishmael's destiny is shaped by Abraham's prayer when he prayed, "O that Ishmael might live before thee!"

What a remarkable story is that of Abraham's standing before God repeating his intercessions for the wicked city of Sodom, the home of his nephew Lot, doomed by God's decision to destroy it! Sodom's fate was for a while stayed by Abraham's praying, and was almost entirely relieved by the humility and insistence of the praying of this man who believed strongly in prayer and who knew how to pray. No other recourse was opened to Abraham to save Sodom but prayer. Perhaps the failure to ultimately rescue Sodom from her doom of destruction was due to Abraham's optimistic view of the spiritual condition of things in that city. It might have been possible,—who knows?—that if Abraham had entreated God once more, and asked Him to spare the city if even one righteous man was found there, for Lot's sake, He might have heeded Abraham's request.

Note another instance in the life of Abraham as showing how he was a man of prayer and had power with God. Abraham had journeyed to and was sojourning in Gerar. Fearing that Abimelech might kill him and appropriate Sarah his wife to his own lustful uses, he deceived Abimelech by claiming that Sarah was his sister. God appeared unto Abimelech in a dream and warned him not to touch Sarah, telling him that she was the wife of Abraham, and not his sister. Then he said unto Abimelech, "Now restore therefore the man his wife; for he is a prophet, and he shall pray for thee, and thou shalt live." And the conclusion of the incident is thus recorded: "So Abraham prayed unto God, and God healed Abimelech and his wife, and his maid servants, and they bare children. For the Lord had fast closed up all the wombs of the house of Abimelech because of Sarah, his wife."

This was a case somewhat on the line of that of Job at the close of his fearful experience and his terrible trials, when his friends, not understanding Job, neither comprehending God's dealings with this servant of His, falsely charged Job with being in sin as the cause of all his troubles. God said to these friends

Application to My Life:

of Job, "My servant Job shall pray for you, for him will I accept. And the Lord turned the captivity of Job when he had prayed for his friends."

Almighty God knew His servant Job as a man of prayer, and He could afford to send these friends of Job to him to pray in order to carry out and fulfill His plans and purposes.

It was Abraham's rule to stand before the Lord in prayer. His life was surcharged with prayer and Abraham's dispensation was sanctified by prayer. For wherever he halted in his pilgrimage, prayer was his inseparable accompaniment. Side by side with the altar of sacrifice was the altar of prayer. He got up early in the morning to the place where he stood before the Lord in prayer.

Chapter 4

Moses, The Mighty Intercessor

Intercessory Prayer is a powerful means of grace to the praying man. Martyn observes that at times of inward dryness and depression, he had often found a delightful revival in the act of praying for others for their conversion, or sanctification, or prosperity in the work of the Lord. His dealings with God for them about these gifts and blessings were for himself the divinely natural channel of a renewed insight into his own part and lot in Christ, into Christ as his own rest and power, into the "perfect freedom" of an entire yielding of himself to his Master for His work.

—Bishop Handley C. G. Moule

Prayer unites with the purposes of God and lays itself out to secure those purposes. How often would the wise and benign will of God fail in its rich and beneficent ends by the sins of the people if prayer had not come in to arrest wrath and make the promise sure! Israel as a nation would have met their just destruction and their just fate after their apostasy with the golden calf had it not been for the interposition and unfainting importunity of Moses' forty days' and forty nights' praying!

Marvelous was the effect of the character of Moses by his marvelous praying. His near and sublime intercourse with God in the giving of the law worked no transfiguration of character like the tireless praying of those forty days in prayer with God. It was when he came down from that long struggle of prayer that his face shone with such dazzling brightness. Our mounts of transfiguration and the heavenly shining in character and conduct are born of seasons of wrestling prayer. All-night

Application to My Life:

praying has changed many a Jacob, the supplanter, into Israel, a prince, who has power with God and with men.

No mission was more majestic in purpose and results than that of Moses, and none was more responsible, diligent and difficult. In it we are taught the sublime ministry and rule of prayer. Not only is it the medium of supply and support, but it is a compassionate agency through which the pitying long-suffering of God has an outflow. Prayer is a medium to restrain God's wrath, that mercy might rejoice against judgment.

Moses himself and his mission were the creation of prayer. Thus it is recorded: "When Jacob was come into Egypt, and your fathers cried unto the Lord, then the Lord sent Moses and Aaron, who brought your fathers out of Egypt, and made them dwell in this place." This is the genesis of the great movement for the deliverance of the Hebrews from Egyptian bondage.

The great movements of God have had their origin and energy in and were shaped by prayers of men. Prayer has directly to deal with God. Other ends, collateral and incidental, are secured by prayer, but mainly, almost solely, prayer has to deal with God. He is pleased to order His policy, and base His action on the prayers of His saints. Prayer influences God greatly. Moses cannot do God's great work, though God-commissioned, without praying much. Moses cannot govern God's people and carry out the divine plans, without having his censer filled full of the incense of prayer. The work of God cannot be done without the fire and fragrance are always burning, ascending and perfuming.

Moses' prayers are often found relieving the terrible stroke of God's wrath. Four times were the prayers of Moses solicited by Pharaoh to relieve him of the fearful stroke of God's wrath. "Entreat the Lord," most earnestly begged Pharaoh of Moses, while the loathsome frogs were upon him. And "Moses cried unto the Lord because of the frogs which God had brought against the land of Egypt, and the Lord did according to the word of Moses." When the grievous plague of flies had corrupted the whole land, Pharaoh again piteously cried out to Moses, "Entreat for me." Moses went out from Pharaoh and entreated the Lord, and the Lord again did according to the word of Moses. The mighty thunderings and hail in their alarming and destructive fury extorted from this wicked king the very same earnest appeal to Moses, "Entreat the Lord." And Moses went out from the city into privacy, and alone with Almighty God, he "spread abroad his hands unto the Lord, and the thunderings and hail ceased, and the rain was not poured out upon the earth."

Application to My Life:

Though Moses was the man of law, yet with him prayer asserted its mighty force. With him, as in the more spiritual dispensation, it could have been said, "My house is the house of prayer."

Moses accepts at its full face value the foundation principle of praying that prayer has to do with God. With Abraham we saw this dearly and strongly enunciated. With Moses it is dearer and stronger still if possible. It declared that prayer affected God, that God was influenced in His conduct by prayer, and that God hears and answer prayer even when the hearing and answering might change His conduct and reverse His action. Stronger than all other laws, and more inflexible than any other decree, is the decree, "Call upon me and I will answer you."

Moses lived near God, and had the freest and most unhindered and boldest access to God, but this, instead of abating the necessity of prayer, made it more necessary, obvious and powerful. Familiarity and closeness to God gives relish, frequency, point and potency to prayer. Those who know God the best are the richest and most powerful in prayer. Little acquaintance with God, and strangeness and coldness to Him, make prayer a rare and feeble thing.

There were conditions of extremity to which Moses was reduced which prayer did not relieve, but there is no position of extremity which baffles God, when prayer pats God into the matter.

Moses' mission was a divine one. It was ordered, directed and planned by God. The more there is of God in a movement, the more there is of prayer, conspicuous and controlling. Moses' prayer rule of the church illustrates the necessity of courage and persistence in prayer. For forty days and forty nights was Moses pressing his prayer for the salvation of the Lord's people. So intense was his concern for them which accompanied his long season of praying, that bodily infirmities and appetites were retired. How strangely the prayers of a righteous man affect God is evident from the exclamation of God to Moses, "Now, therefore, let me alone, that my wrath may wax hot against them, that I may consume them; and I will make of thee a great nation." The presence of such an influence over God fills us with astonishment, awe and fear. How lofty, bold and devoted must be such a pleader!

Read this from the divine record:

"And Moses returned unto the Lord, and said, Oh, this people have sinned a great sin, and have made them gods of gold!

"Yet now if thou wilt forgive their sin—and if not, blot me, I pray thee, out of thy book which thou hast written.

Application to My Life:

"And the Lord said unto Moses, Whosoever hath sinned against me, him will I blot out of my book.

"Therefore now go, and lead the people unto the place of which I have spoken unto thee. Behold my angel shall go before thee."

The rebellion of Korah was the occasion of God's anger flaming out against the whole congregation of Israel, who sympathized with these rebels. Again Moses appears on the stage of action, this time having Aaron to join him in intercession for these sinners against God. But it only shows that in a serious time like this Moses knew to whom to go for relief, and was encouraged to pray that God would stay His wrath and spare Israel. Here is what is said about the matter:

"And the Lord spake unto Moses and Aaron, saying,

"Separate yourselves from among this congregation, that I may consume them in a moment.

"And they fell on their faces, and said, O God, the God of the spirits of all flesh, shall one man sin, and wilt thou be wroth with all the congregation?"

The assumption, pride and rebellion of Miriam, sister of Moses, in which she had the presence and sympathy of Aaron, put the praying and the spirit of Moses in the noblest and most amiable light. Because of her sin God smote her with leprosy. But Moses made tender and earnest intercession for his sister who had so grievously offended God, and his prayer saved her from the fearful and incurable malady.

The record is intensely interesting, and follows just here:

"And the anger of the Lord was kindled against them and the cloud departed from off the tabernacle and behold, Miriam became

leprous, white as snow; and Aaron looked upon Miriam, and behold she was leprous.

"And Aaron said unto Moses, Alas, my Lord, I beseech thee, lay not the sin unto us, wherein we have done foolishly, and wherein we have sinned.

"Let her not be as one dead, of whom the flesh is half consumed when he cometh out of his mother's womb.

"And Moses cried unto the Lord, saying, Heal her, O God, I beseech thee.

"And the Lord said unto Moses, If her father had but spit in her face, should she not be ashamed seven days? Let her be shut out from the camp seven days, and after that let her be received again."

The murmurings of the children of Israel furnished conditions which called into play the full forces of prayer.

Application to My Life:

They impressively bring out the intercessory feature of prayer and disclose Moses in his great office as an intercessor before God in behalf of others. It was at Marah, where the waters were bitter and the people grievously murmured against Moses and God.

Here is the Scripture account:

"And when they came to Marah, they could not drink of the waters of Marah; for they were bitter; therefore the name of it was called Marah.

"And the people murmured against Moses, saying, What shall we drink?

"And Moses cried unto the Lord; and the Lord showed him a tree, which when he had cast into the waters, the waters were made sweet; there he made for them a statute and an ordinance, and there he proved them."

How many of the bitter places of the earth have been sweetened by prayer the records of eternity alone will disclose.

Again at Taberah the people complained, and God became angry with them, and Moses came again to the front and stepped into the breach and prayed for them. Here is the brief account:

"And when the people complained, it displeased the Lord; and the Lord heard it; and his anger was kindled; and the fire of the Lord burnt among them, and consumed them that were in the uttermost part of the camp.

"And the people cried unto Moses, and when unto the Lord, the fire was quenched."

Moses got what he asked for. His praying was specific and God's answer was likewise specific. Always was he heard by

Almighty God when prayed, and always was he answered by God. Once the answer was not specific. He had prayed to go into Canaan. The answer came but not what he asked for. He was given a vision of the Promised Land, but he was not allowed to go over Jordan into that land of promise. It was a prayer on the order of Paul's when he prayed three times for the removal of the thorn in the flesh. But the thorn was not removed. Grace, however, was vouchsafed which made the thorn a blessing.

It must not be thought that because Psalm 90 is incorporated with what is known as the "Psalms of David," that David was the author of it. By general consent it is attributed to Moses, and it gives us a sample of the praying of this giver of the law of God to the people. It is a prayer worth studying. It is sacred to us because it has been the requiem uttered over our dead for years that are past and gone. It has blessed the grave of many a sleeping saint. But its very familiarity may cause us to lose its

Application to My Life:

full meaning. Wise will we be if we digest it, not for the dead, but for the living, that it may teach us how to live, how to pray while living, and how to die. "So teach us to number our days that we may apply our hearts to wisdom. Establish thou the work of our hands, yea, the work of our hands establish thou it."

Chapter 5

Elijah, The Praying Prophet

"I have known men," says Goodwin—it must have been himself—"who came to God for nothing else but just to come to Him, they so loved Him. They scorned to soil Him and themselves with any other errand than just purely to be alone with Him in His presence. Friendship is best kept up, even among men, by frequent visits; and the more free and defecate those frequent visits are, and the less occasioned by business, or necessity, or custom they are, the more friendly and welcome they are."

—Rev. Alexander Whyte

Elijah is preeminently the elder of the prophets. The crown, the throne and the scepter are his. His garments are white with flame. He seems exalted in his fiery and prayerful nature, as a being seemingly superhuman, but the New Testament places him alongside of us as man of like nature with us. Instead of placing himself outside the sphere of humanity, in the marvelous results of his praying, it points to him as an example to be imitated and as inspiration to stimulate us. To pray like Elijah, and to have results like Elijah, is the crying need of the times.

Elijah had learned the lesson of prayer, and had graduated in that divine school ere we know him. Somewhere in the secret places, on mountain or in plain, he had been alone with God, an intercessor against the debasing idolatry of Ahab. Mightily had his prayers prevailed with God. How confidently and well assured were the answers to his praying.

Application to My Life:

He had been talking with God about vengeance. He was the embodiment of his times. Those times were times of vengeance. The intercessor was not to be clothed with an olive branch with its fillet of wood, the symbol of a suppliant for mercy, but with fire, the symbol of justice and the messenger of wrath. How abruptly does he come before us in the presence of Ahab! Well assured and with holy boldness does he declare before the astonished, cowering king his message of fearful import, a message gained by his earnest praying,—"in praying he prayed that it might not rain," and God did not deny his prayer. "As the Lord God of Israel liveth, before whom I stand, there shall not be dew nor rain these years but according to my word."

The secret of his praying and the character of the man are found in the words, "Before whom I stand." We are here reminded of Gabriel's words to Zacharias in informing this priest of the coming of a son to him and his wife in their old age: "I am Gabriel that standeth in the presence of God." The archangel Gabriel had scarcely more unflinching devotion, more courage, and more readiness of obedience, and more jealously of God's honor, than Elijah. What projecting power do we see in his prayer! "And it rained not on the earth by the space of three years and six months." What omnipotent forces which can command the powers of nature! "Not dew nor rain." What man is this who dares utter such a claim or assert such a power? If his claim be false, he is a fanatic or a madman. If his claim be true, he has stayed the benevolent arm of Omnipotence, and put himself, by God's leave, in God's place. The accursed and burnt-up land and the fiery, rainless and dewless days and nights, attest the truth of his saying, and prove the sternness, strength, firmness and passion of the man who holds back the clouds and stays the blessed visitation of the rain. Elijah is his name, and this attests the truth of that name, "My God is Jehovah."

His prayers have the power to stay the benignant course of nature. He stands in God's stead in this matter. The sober, passionless, unimaginative James, the brother of our Lord, in his Epistle, says to us: "See what prayer can do, by Elijah! Pray as Elijah prayed. Let the righteous man put forth to its fullest extent the energy of prayer. Let saints and sinners, angels and devils, see and feel the mighty potencies of prayer. See how the prayer of a good man has power and influence, and avails with God!"

No sham praying was that of Elijah, no mere performance, no spiritless, soulless, official praying was it. Elijah was in Elijah's praying. The whole man, with all his fiery forces, was in it. Almighty God to him was real. Prayer to him was the means

Application to My Life:

of projecting God in full force on the world, in order to vindicate His name, establish His own being, to avenge His blasphemed name and violated law, and to vindicate His servants.

Instead of "prayed earnestly," in James 5:17, the Revised Version has it, "In his prayer he prayed," or "with prayer he prayed." That is, with all the combined energies of prayer he prayed.

Elijah's praying was strong, insistent, and resistless in its elements of power. Feeble praying secures no results and brings neither glory to God nor good to man.

Elijah learned new and higher lessons of prayer while hidden away by God and with God when he was by the brook Cherith. He was doubtless communing with God while Ahab was searching all lands for him. After a while he was ordered to Sarepta, where God had commanded a widow to sustain him. He went there for the widow's good as well as for his own. A benefit to Elijah and a signal good to the widow were the results of Elijah's going. While this woman provided for him, he provided for the woman. Elijah's prayers did more for the woman than the woman's hospitality did for Elijah. Great trials awaited the widow and great sorrows too. Her widowhood and her poverty tell of her struggles and her sorrows. Elijah was there to relieve her poverty and to assuage her griefs.

Here is the interesting account:

"And it came to pass that after these things, the son of the woman, the mistress of the house, fell sick; and his sickness was sore, that there was no breath left in him.

"And she said unto Elijah, What have I do to with thee, O thou man of God? Art thou come unto me to call my sin to remembrance and to slay my son?

"*And he said unto her, Give me thy son. And he took him out of her bosom, and carried him up into a loft, where he abode, and laid him upon his own bed.*

"*And he cried unto the Lord, and said, O Lord my God, hast thou also brought evil upon the widow with whom I sojourn by slaying her son?*

"*And he stretched himself upon the child three times, and cried unto the Lord, and said, O Lord my God, I pray thee let this child's soul come into him again.*

"*And the Lord heard the voice of Elijah, and the soul of the child came into him again, and he revived.*

"*And Elijah took the child and brought him down out of the chamber into the house, and delivered him unto his mother. And Elijah said, See, thy son liveth.*

Application to My Life:

"And the woman said to Elijah, Now by this I know that thou art a man of God, and that the word of the Lord in thy mouth is truth."

Elijah's prayer enters regions where prayer had never gone before. The awful, mysterious and powerful regions of the dead are now invaded by the presence and demands of prayer. Jesus Christ refers to Elijah's going to this widow as mainly, if not solely, for her good. Elijah's presence and praying keep the woman from starving and brings her son back from death. Surely no sorrow is like the bitterness of the loss of an only son. With what assured confidence Elijah faces the conditions! There is no hesitancy in his actions, and there is no pause in his faith. He takes the dead son to his own room, and alone with God he makes the issue. In that room God meets him and the struggle is with God alone. The struggle is too intense and too sacred for companionship or for spectator. The prayer is made to God and the issue is with God. The child has been taken by God, and God rules in the realms of death. In His hands are the issues of life and death. Elijah believed that God had taken the child's spirit, and that God could as well restore that spirit. God answered Elijah's prayer. The answer was the proof of Elijah's mission from God, and of the truth of God's Word. The dead child brought to life was a sure conviction of this truth: "Now by this I know that thou art a man of God, and that the word of the Lord in thy mouth is truth. Answers to prayer are the evidences of the being of God and of the truth of His Word.

The immortal test of Elijah made in the presence of an apostate king, and in the face of a backslidden nation and an idolatrous priesthood on Mount Carmel, is a sublime exhibition of faith and prayer. In the contest the prophets of Baal had failed. No fire from heaven falls from heaven in answer to their frantic cries. Elijah, in great quietness of spirit and with confident assurance, calls Israel to him. He repairs the wasted altar of God, the altar of sacrifice and of prayer, and puts the pieces of the bullock in order on the altar. He then uses every preventive against any charge of deception. Every thing is flooded with water. Then Elijah prays a model prayer, remarkable for its clearness, its simplicity and its utmost candor. It is noted for its brevity and its faith.

Read the account given in the Scriptures:

"And it came to pass at the time of the offering of the evening sacrifice, that Elijah the prophet came near and said, Lord God of Abraham, Isaac and of Israel, let it be known this day that thou art God in Israel, and that I am thy servant, and that I have done all these things at thy word.

"Hear me, O Lord, hear me, that this people may know that thou art the Lord God, and that thou hast turned their heart back again.

Application to My Life:

"Then the fire of the Lord fell, and consumed the burnt sacrifice, and the wood, and the stones, and the dust, and licked up the water that was in the trench.

"And when all the people saw it, they fell on their faces; and they said, The Lord, He is God; The Lord, He is God."

Elijah had been dealing directly with God as before. True prayer always deals with God. This prayer of Elijah was to determine the existence of the true God, and the answer direct from God settles the question. The answer is also the credentials of Elijah's divine mission and the evidence that God deals with men. If we had more of Elijah's praying, marvels would not be the marvels that they are now to us. God would not be so strange, so far away in being and so feeble in action. Everything is tame and feeble because our praying is so tame and feeble.

God said to Elijah, "Go show thyself to Ahab, and I will send rain on the earth." Elijah acted promptly on the divine order, and showed himself to Ahab. He had made his issue with Ahab, Israel and Baal. The whole current of national feeling had turned back to God. The day was fading into the evening shades. No rain had come. But Elijah did not fold his arms and say the promise had failed, but gave point and fulfillment to the promise.

Here is the Scripture record with the result given:

"And Elijah said unto Ahab, Get thee up, eat and drink, for there is a sound of abundance of rain.

"So Ahab went up to eat and to drink. And Elijah went up to the top of Carmel. And he cast himself down upon the earth, and put his face between his knees.

"And said to his servant, Go up now, look toward the sea. And he went up and looked, and said, There is nothing. And he said, Go again seven times.

"And it came to pass at the seventh time that he said, Behold there riseth a little cloud out of the sea, like a man's hand. And he said, Go up, say unto Ahab, Prepare thy chariot, and get thee down, that the rain stop thee not.

"And it came to pass in the meanwhile, that the heaven was black with clouds and wind, and there was a great rain. And Ahab rode and went to Jezreel.

"And the hand of the Lord was on Elijah."

Then it was, as James records, "And he prayed again, and the heaven gave rain, and the earth brought forth her fruit."

Application to My Life:

Elijah's importunate, fiery praying and God's promise brought the rain. Prayer carries the promise to its gracious fulfillment. It takes persistent and persevering prayer to give to the promise its largest and most gracious results. In this instance it was expectant prayer, watchful of results, looking for the answer. Elijah had the answer in the small cloud like a man's hand. He had the inward assurance of the answer even before he had the rain. How Elijah's praying shames our feeble praying! His praying brought things to pass. It vindicated the existence and being of God, brought conviction to dull and sluggish consciences, and proved that God was still God in the nation. Elijah's praying turned a whole nation back to God, ordered the moving of the clouds, and directed the falling of the rain. It called down fire from heaven to prove the existence of God or to destroy God's enemies.

The praying of the Elder Prophet of Israel was clothed in his robes of fire. The golden crown was on his head, and his censer was full and fragrant with the flame, the melody and the perfume of prayer. What wonderful power clothed him on this occasion! It was no wonder that Elisha cried out as he saw this fiery prophet of the Lord enter the chariot for his heavenly ride, "My father! my father! The chariot of Israel and the horsemen thereof!" But chariots and armies could not begin to do as much for Israel as did this praying Elijah. Prayers are omnipotent forces, worldwide and heaven-reaching.

Where are the praying ones of modern times of fiery faith who can incense Elijah's prayers? We need at this time rulers in the Church who can add to the force, flame and fragrance of Elijah's praying by their own prayers.

Elijah could touch nothing but by prayer. God was with him mightily because he was mighty in prayer.

In the contest with the prophets of Baal, he makes the issue clearly and positively to determine the true God, as one to be made by prayer. Does God live? Is the Bible a revelation from Him? How often in these days are those questions rising? How often do they need to be settled? An appeal by prayer is the only Settlement to them. Where is the trouble? Not in God, but in our praying. The proof of God and of His being is that He answers prayer. It takes the faith and prayer of Elijah to settle the question. Where are the Elijahs in the Church of the present day? Where are the men of like passions as he, who can pray as he prayed? We have thousands of men of like passions, but where are the men of like praying as he was? Notice with what calm, assured confidence he stakes the issue and builds the altar. How calm and pointed is his prayer on that occasion!

Instead of such praying being out of the range of New Testament principles and moderation, this very praying of

Application to My Life:

Elijah is pressed as an example to be imitated and as an illustration of what prayer can do when performed by the right men in the right way. Elijah's results could be secured if we had more Elijah men to do the praying.

Elijah prayed really, truly and earnestly. How much of praying there is at the present time which is not real praying, but is a mere shell, shucks, and mere words! Much of it might well be termed non-praying. The world is full of such praying. It goes nowhere, it avails nothing, it brings no returns. In fact, no returns nor results are expected.

The requisites of true prayer are the requisites of scriptural, vital, personal religion. They are the requisites of real religious service in this life. Primary among these requisites is that in serving, we serve. So in praying, we must pray. Truth and heart reality, these are the core, the substance, the sum, the heart of prayer. There are no possibilities in prayer without we really pray in all simplicity, reality and trueness. Prayerless praying—how common, how popular, how delusive and vain!

Chapter 6

Hezekiah, The Praying King

One can form a habit of study until the will seems to be at rest and only the intellect is engaged, the will having retired altogether from exercise. This is not true of real praying. If the affections are laggard, cold, indifferent, if the intellect is furnishing no material to clothe the petition with imagery and fervor, the prayer is a mere vaporing of intellectual exercise, nothing being accomplished worth while.

—Rev. Homer W. Hodge

The great religious reformation under King Hezekiah and the prophet Isaiah was thoroughly impregnated with prayer in its various stages. King Hezekiah, of Judah, will serve as an illustration of a praying elder of God's Church, white-robed and gold-crowned. He had genius and strength, wisdom and piety. He was a statesman, a general, a poet and a religious reformer. He is a distinct surprise to us, not so much because of his strength and genius—they were to be expected—but in his piety, under all the circumstances connected with him. The rare statement, "He did that which was right in the sight of the Lord," is a glad and thrilling surprise when we consider all his antecedents and his environments. Where did he come from? Under what circumstances was his childhood life spent? Who were his parents and what were their religious character? Worldliness, half-heartedness and utter apostasy marked the reign of his father, grandfather and his great-grandfather. His

Application to My Life:

home surroundings as he grew up were far from being favorable to godliness and faith in God. One thing, however, favored him. He was fortunate in having Isaiah for his friend and counselor when he assumed the crown of Judah. How much there is in a ruler's having a God-fearing man for a counselor and an associate!

With what familiar and successful praying did he intercede with God is seen in the Passover feast, in which a number of the people were unfitted to participate. They had not prepared themselves by the required ceremonial cleansing, and it was important that they be allowed to eat the Passover feast with all the others.

Here is the brief account with special reference to the praying of Hezekiah and the result:

"For there were many in the congregation that were not sanctified; therefore the Levites had the charge of the killing of the passover for every one that was not clean, to sanctify them unto the Lord.

"For a multitude of the people had not cleansed themselves yet did they eat the passover otherwise than it was written. But Hezekiah prayed for them saying, The Good Lord pardon every one.

"That prepareth his heart to seek God, the Lord God of his fathers, though he be not cleansed according to the purification of the sanctuary.

"And the Lord hearkened to Hezekiah, and healed the people."

So the Lord heard him as he prayed, and even the violation of the most sacred law of the Passover was forgiven in answer to the prayer of this praying, God-fearing king. Law must yield its scepter to prayer.

The strength, directness and foundation of his faith and prayer are found in his words to his army. Memorable words are they, stronger and mightier than all the hosts of Sennacherib:

"Be strong and courageous; be not afraid nor dismayed for the king of Assyria, nor for all the multitude that is with him; for there be more with us than with him.

"With him is an arm of flesh; but with us is the Lord our God to help us, and to fight our battles. And the people rested themselves upon the words of Hezekiah, king of Judah."

His defense against the mighty enemies of God was prayer. His enemies quailed and were destroyed his prayers

Application to My Life:

when his own armies were powerless. God's people were always safe when their princes were princes in prayer.

An occasion of serious import came to the people of God during his reign which was to test his faith in God and furnish opportunity to try the prayer agency to obtain deliverance. Judah was sorely pressed by the Assyrians, and, humanly speaking, defeat and captivity seemed imminent. The King of Assyria sent a commission to defy and blaspheme the name of God and to insult King Hezekiah, and they uttered their insults and blasphemy publicly. Note what Hezekiah immediately did without hesitation:

"And it came to pass when King Hezekiah heard it, that he rent his clothes and covered himself with sackcloth, and went into the house of the Lord."

His very first impression was to turn to God by going to the "house of prayer." God was in his thoughts, and prayer was the first thing to be done. And so he sent messengers to Isaiah to join him in prayer. In such an emergency God must not be left out of the account. God must be appealed to for deliverance from these blasphemous enemies of God and His people.

Just at this particular juncture the forces of the King of Assyria, which were besieging Hezekiah, were diverted from an immediate attack on Jerusalem. The King of Assyria, however, sent to Hezekiah a defaming and blasphemous letter.

For the second time, as he is insulted and beset by the forces of this heathen king, he enters the house of the Lord, the "house of prayer." Where else should he go? And to whom should he appeal but unto the God of Israel?

"And Hezekiah received the letter from the hand of the messengers, and read it; and Hezekiah went up to the house of the Lord, and spread it before the Lord.

"And Hezekiah prayed unto the Lord: O Lord of hosts, the God of Israel that dwellest between the cherubim, Thou art the God, even thou alone, of all the kingdoms of the earth. Thou hast made heaven and earth.

"Now, therefore, O Lord our God, save us from his hand, that all the kingdoms of the earth may know that thou art the Lord, even thou only."

And note the speedy answer and the marvelous results of such praying by this God-fearing king. First, Isaiah gave the King full assurance that he need fear nothing. God had heard the prayer, and would give a great deliverance.

Application to My Life:

Then secondly, the angel of the Lord came with swift wings and smote 185,000 Assyrians. The king was vindicated, God was honored, and the people of God were saved.

The united prayer. of the praying king and of the praying prophet were almighty forces in bringing deliverance and destroying God's enemies. Armies lay at their mercy, defenceless; and angels, swift-winged and armed with almighty power and vengeance, were their allies.

Hezekiah had ministered in prayer in destroying idolatry and in reforming his kingdom. In meeting his enemies, prayer had been his chief weapon. He now comes to try its efficiency against the set and declared purposes of Almighty God. Will it avail in this new field of action? Let us see. Hezekiah was very sick, and God sends his own familiar friend and wise counselor and prophet, Isaiah, to warn him of his approaching end, and to tell him to arrange all his affairs for his final departure. This is the Scriptural statement:

"In those days was Hezekiah sick unto death. And the Prophet Isaiah, the son of Amoz, came to him, and said unto him, Thus saith the Lord: Set thy house in order, for thou shalt die and not live."

The decree came direct from God that he should die. What can set aside or reverse that Divine decree of heaven? Hezekiah had never been in a condition so insuperable with a decree so direct and definite from God. Can prayer change the purposes of God? Can prayer snatch from the jaws of death one who has been decreed to die? Can prayer save a man from an incurable sickness? These were the questions with which his faith had now to deal. But his faith does not seem to pause one moment. His faith is not staggered one minute at the sudden and definite news conveyed to him by the Lord's prophet. No such questions which modern unbelief or disbelief would raise are started in his mind. At once he gives himself to prayer. Immediately without delay he applies to God who issued the edict. To whom else could he go? Cannot God change His own purposes if He chooses?

Note what Hezekiah did in this emergency, sorely pressed, and see the gracious result:

"Then he turned his face to the wall and prayed unto the Lord, saying,

"I beseech thee, O Lord, remember now how I have walked before thee in truth and with a perfect heart, and have done that which is good in thy sight. And Hezekiah wept sore."

It was no self-righteous plea which he offered to God for recovery. He was only pleading his fidelity, just as Christ did in after years:

"Father I have glorified thee on earth."

Application to My Life:

_____

_____

_____

_____

_____

_____

_____

_____

_____

_____

_____

_____

He is the Lord's reminder, and is putting Him in mind as to his sincerity, fidelity and service, which was in every way legitimate. This prayer was directly in line with that of David in Psalm 26:1, "Judge me, O Lord, for I have walked in my integrity." This is not a prayer test with Hezekiah, nor is it a faith cure, but it is a testing of God. It must be God's cure if a cure comes at all.

Hezekiah had hardly finished his prayer, and Isaiah was just about to go home when God gave him another message for Hezekiah, this time one more pleasant and encouraging. The mighty force of prayer had affected God, and had changed His edict and reversed Him in His purpose concerning Hezekiah. What is that which prayer cannot do? What is it which a praying man cannot accomplish through prayer?

"And it came to pass before Isaiah had gone out into the middle court, that the word of the Lord came to him, saying,

"Turn again, and tell Hezekiah, the captain of my people, Thus, saith the Lord, the God of David thy father, I have heard thy prayer; I have seen thy tears; Behold, I will heal thee; on the third day thou shalt go up to the house of the Lord.

"And I will add unto thy days fifteen years, and I will deliver thee and this city out of the hand of the King of Assyria; and I will defend this city for my own sake, and for David, my servant's sake."

The prayer was to God. It was that God should reconsider and change His mind. Doubtless Isaiah returned to his house with a lighter heart than he did when he delivered his original message. God had been prayed to by this sick king, and had been asked to revoke His decree, and God had condescended to grant the request. God sometimes changes His mind. He has a right to do so. The reasons for Him to change His mind are strong reasons. His servant Hezekiah wants it done. Hezekiah had been a dutiful servant and had done much for God. Truth, perfection and goodness have been the elements of Hezekiah's service and the rule of his life. Hezekiah's tears and prayer are in the way of God's executing His decree to take away the life of His servant. Prayer and tears are mighty things with God. They are to Him much more than consistency and much more to Him than decrees. "I have heard thy prayer; I have seen thy tears; behold I will heal thee."

Sickness dies before prayer. Health comes in answer to prayer. God answered more than Hezekiah asked for. Hezekiah prayed only for his life, and God gave him life and in addition promised him protection and security from his enemies.

But Isaiah had something to do with the recovery of this praying king. There was something more than prayer in it.

Application to My Life:

Isaiah's praying was changed into the skill of the physician. "And Isaiah said, Take a lump of figs. And they took and laid it on the boil, and he recovered."

God often uses remedies in answering prayer. It frequently takes a stronger faith to rise above means and not to trust in them, than it does to wholly reject all means. Here was a simple remedy that all might know that it did not cure the deadly disease, and yet a means to aid or to test faith. But still more praying was to be done. Isaiah and Hezekiah could not do things without much praying:

"And Hezekiah said unto Isaiah, What shall be the sign that the Lord will heal me, and that I shall go up into the house of the Lord the third day?

"And Isaiah said, This sign shalt thou have of the Lord, that the Lord will do the thing that he hath spoken: Shall the shadow go forward ten degrees, or go back ten degrees?

"And Hezekiah answered, It is a light thing for the shadow to go down ten degrees; nay, but let the shadow return backward ten degrees.

"And Isaiah the prophet cried unto the Lord, and he brought the shadow ten degrees backward, by which it had gone down in the dial of Ahaz."

Hezekiah meets the occasion and covers the answer to his prayer with thanksgiving. The fragrance of the sweet spices are there, and the melody of the harp also.

Four things let us ever keep in mind: God hears prayer, God heeds prayer, God answers prayer, and God delivers by prayer. These things cannot be too often repeated. Prayer breaks all bars, dissolves all chains, opens all prisons and widens all straits by which God's saints have been holden.

Life was sweet to Hezekiah and he desired to live, but what can break God's decree? Nothing but the energy of faith. Hezekiah's heart was broken under the strain, and its waters flowed and added force and volume to his praying. He pleaded with great strivings and with strong arguments; and God heard Hezekiah praying, saw his tears, and changed his mind, and Hezekiah lived to praise God and to be an example of the power of mighty praying.

Like Hezekiah, the decent, soulless way of praying did not suit Paul. He puts himself in the attitude of a wrestler, and charges his brethren to join him in the agony of a great conflict. "Brethren, I beseech you," he says, "for the Lord Jesus Christ's sake, and for the love of the Spirit, that ye strive together with me in your prayers to God for me." He was too much in earnest to touch the praying business genteelly or with gloved hands. He was in it as an agony, and he desired his brethren to be his

Application to My Life:

partners in this conflict and wrestling of his soul. Epaphras was doing this same kind of praying for the Colossians: "Always laboring fervently for you in prayers, that ye may stand perfect and complete in all the will of God." An end worth agonizing for always. This kind of praying by these early pastors of the Apostolic Church was one secret of the purity, one source of the power of the Church. And this was the kind of praying which was done by Hezekiah.

Here was prayer born in the fire of a great desire, and pursued through the deepest agony of conflict and opposition to success. Our spiritual cravings are not strong enough to give life to the mighty conflicts of prayer? They are not absorbing enough to stop business, arrest worldly pursuits, awaken us before day, and send us to the closet, to solitude, and to God; to conquer every opposing force and win our victories from the very jaws of hell. We want preachers and men and women who can illustrate the uses, the forces, the blessing, and the utmost limits of prayer.

Isaiah laments that there was no one who stirred himself up to take hold of God. Much praying was done, but it was too easy, indifferent, complacent. There were no mighty movements of the soul toward God, no array of all the sanctified energies to reach out and grapple God and draw out his treasures for spiritual uses. Forceless prayers have no power to overcome difficulties, no power to win marked results, or gain a complete and wonderful victory.

Chapter 7

Ezra, The Praying Reformer

Before the Great War there were many signs of a new interest in PRAYER and new hope from its exercise. How these signs have multiplied is known to every one. This one thing at least that is good the War has done for us already. Let us not miss our opportunity. Prayer is not an easy exercise. It requires encouragement, exposition, and training. There never was a time when men and women were more sincerely anxious to be told how to pray. Prayer is the mightiest instrument in our armory, and if we are to use it as God has given the encouragement, we must do everything in our power to bring it into exercise.

—Rev. James Hastings

Ezra, the priest, and one of God's great reformers, comes before us in the Old Testament as a praying man, one who uses prayer to overcome difficulties and bring good things to pass. He had returned from Babylon under the patronage of the King of Babylon, who had been strangely moved toward Ezra and who favored him in many ways. Ezra had been in Jerusalem but a few days when the princes came to him with the distressing information that the people had not separated themselves from the people of that country, and were doing according to the abominations of the heathen nations about them. And that which was worse than all was that the princes and rulers in Israel had been chief in the trespass.

It was a sad state of affairs facing Ezra as he found the Church almost hopelessly involved with the world. God demands of His Church in all ages that it should be separated from the world, a separation so sharp that it amounts to an

Application to My Life:

antagonism. To effect this very end, He put Israel in the Promised Land, and cut them off from other nations by mountains, deserts and seas, and straightway charged them that they should not form any relation with alien nations, neither marital, social nor business.

But Ezra finds the Church at Jerusalem, as he returns from Babylon, paralyzed and hopelessly and thoroughly prostrated by the violation of this principle. They had intermarried, and had formed the closest and most sacred ties in family, social and business life, with the Gentile nations. All were involved in it, priests, Levites, princes and people. The family, the business, and the religious life of the people was founded in this violation of God's law. What was to be done? What could be done? Here were the important questions which faced this leader in Israel, this man of God.

Everything appeared to be against the recovery of the Church. Ezra could not preach to them, because the whole city would be inflamed, and would hound him out of the place. What force was there which could recover them to God so that they would dissolve business partnerships, divorce wives and husbands, cut acquaintances and dissolve friendships?

The first thing about Ezra which is worthy of remark was that he saw the situation and realized how serious it was. He was not a blind-eyed optimist who never sees anything wrong in the Church. By the mouth of Isaiah God had propounded the very pertinent question, "Who is blind but my servant?" But it could not possibly be made to apply to Ezra. Nor did he minimize the condition of things or seek to palliate the sins of the people or to minimize the enormity of their crimes. Their offense appeared in his eyes to be serious in the extreme. It is worth not a little to have leaders in Zion who have eyes to see the sins of the Church as well as the evils of the times. One great need of the modern Church is for leaders after the style of Ezra, who are not blind in their seeing department, and who are willing to see the state of things in the Church and who are not reluctant to open their eyes to the real situation.

Very naturally, seeing these dreadful evils in the Church and in the society of Jerusalem, he was distressed. The sad condition of things grieved him, so much so that he rent his garments, plucked his hair, and sat down astonished. All these things are evidences of his great distress of soul at the terrible state of affairs. Then it was in that frame of mind, concerned, solicitous and troubled in soul, that he gave himself to prayer, to confession of the sins of the people, and to pleading for pardoning mercy at the hands of God. To whom should he go in a time like this but unto the God who hears prayer, who is ready to pardon and who can bring the unexpected thing to pass?

Application to My Life:

He was amazed beyond expression at the wicked conduct of the people, was deeply moved and began to fast and pray. Prayer and fasting always accomplish something. He prays with a broken heart, for there is naught else that he can do. He prays unto God, deeply burdened, prostrate on the ground and weeping, while the whole city unites with him in prayer.

Prayer was the only way to placate God, and Ezra became a great mover in a great work for God, with marvelous results. The whole work, its principles and its results, are summarized by just one verse in Ezra 10:1:

"Now when Ezra had prayed, and had confessed, weeping and casting himself down before the house of God, there assembled unto him out of Israel a very great congregation of men and women and children, for the people wept sore."

There had been mighty, simple and persevering prayer. Intense and prevailing prayer had accomplished its end. Ezra's praying had brought into being and brought forth results in a great work for God. It was mighty praying because it brought Almighty God to do His own work, which was absolutely hopeless from any other source save by prayer and by God. But nothing is hopeless to prayer because nothing is hopelessly to God.

Again we must say that prayer has only to do with God, and is only resultful as it has to do with God. Whatever influence the praying of Ezra had upon himself, its chief, if not its only, results followed because it affected God, and moved Him to do the work.

A great and general repentance followed this praying of Ezra, and there occurred a wonderful reformation in Israel. And Ezra's mourning and his praying were the great factors which had to do with bringing these great things to pass.

So thorough was the revival which occurred that as evidences of its genuineness it is noted that the leaders in Israel came to Ezra with these words:

"We have trespassed against our God, and have taken strange wives of the people of the land. Yet now there is hope in Israel concerning this thing.

"Now therefore let us make a covenant with our God to put away all the wives, and such as are born to them, according to the counsel of my lord, and of those that tremble at the commandment of our God; and let it be done according to the law.

"Arise, for this matter belongeth unto thee. We also will be with thee; be of good courage, and do it."

Application to My Life:

Chapter 8

Nehemiah, The Praying Builder

We care not for your splendid abilities as a minister, or your natural endowment as an orator before men. We are sure that the truth of the matter is this: No one will or can command success and become a real praying soul unless intense application is the price. I am even now convinced that the difference between the saints like Wesley, Fletcher, Edwards, Brainerd, Bramwell, Bounds, and ourselves is energy, perseverance, invincible determination to succeed or die in the attempt. God help us.

—*Rev. Homer W. Hodge*

In enumerating the praying saints of the Old Testament, we must not leave out of that sacred catalogue Nehemiah, the builder. He stands out on an equal footing with the others who have been considered. In the story of the reconstruction of Jerusalem after the captivity, he plays a prominent part, and prayer is prominent in his life during those years. He was a captive in Babylon, and had an important position in the palace of the king to whom he was cup bearer. There must have been considerable merit in him to cause the king to take a Hebrew captive and place him in such an office, where be really had the life of the king in his charge, because he was responsible for the wine which he drank.

It was while Nehemiah was in Babylon, in the king's palace, that one day his brethren came from Jerusalem, and very naturally Nehemiah desired news from the people there and information concerning the city itself. The distressing

Application to My Life:

information was given him that the walls were broken down, the gates were burned with fire, and the remnant who were left there at the beginning of the captivity were in great affliction and reproach.

Just one verse gives the effect of this sad news upon this man of God:

"And it came to pass when I heard these words, that I sat down and wept, and mourned certain days and fasted, and prayed before the God of Heaven."

Here was a man whose heart was in his own native land far away from where he now lived. He loved Israel, was concerned for the welfare of Zion, and was true to God. Deeply distressed by the information concerning his brethren at Jerusalem, he mourned and wept. How few the strong men in these days who can weep at the evils and abominations of the times! How rare those who, seeing the desolations of Zion, are sufficiently interested and concerned for the welfare of the Church to mourn! Mourning and weeping over the decay of religion, the decline of revival power, and the fearful inroads of worldliness in the Church are almost an unknown quantity. There is so much of so-called optimism that leaders have no eyes to see the breaking down of the walls of Zion and the low spiritual state of the Christians of the present day, and have less heart to mourn and cry about it. Nehemiah was a mourner in Zion. And possessing this state of heart, distressed beyond measure, he does that which other praying saints had done—he goes to God and makes it a subject of prayer. The prayer is recorded in Nehemiah 1, and is a model after which to pattern our prayers. He begins with adoration, makes confession of the sins of his nation, pleads the promises of God, mentions former mercies, and begs for pardoning mercy. Then with an eye to the future—

for unquestionably he had planned, the next time he was summoned into the King's presence, to ask permission to visit Jerusalem and to do there what was possible to remedy the distressing state of affairs—we hear him pray for something very special: "And prosper thy servant this day, I pray thee, and grant him mercy in the sight of this man. For," he adds by way of explanation, "I was the king's cup bearer."

It seemed all right to pray for his people, but how was a heathen king, with possibly no sympathy whatever for the sad condition of his city and his people in a captive land, and who had no interest in the matter, to be so favorably affected that he would consent to give up his faithful cup bearer and allow him to be gone for months? But Nehemiah believed in a God who could touch even the mind of a heathen ruler and move him favorably toward the request of his praying servant.

Application to My Life:

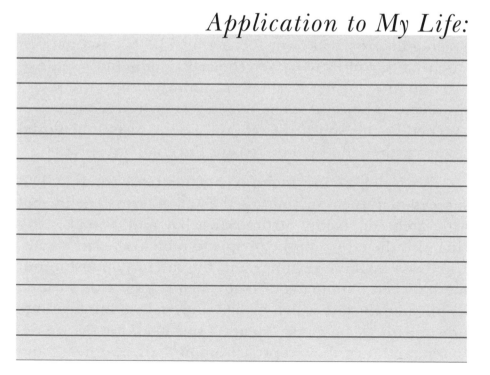

Nehemiah was summoned into the king's presence, and God used even the appearance of Nehemiah's countenance as an entering wedge to gain the consent of Artaxerxes. This started the inquiry of the king as to its cause, and the final result was that the king not only permitted Nehemiah to go back to Jerusalem but furnished him with everything needful for the journey and for the success of the enterprise.

Nor did Nehemiah rest his ease when he first prayed about this matter, but he stated this significant fact as he was talking to the king: "So I prayed unto the God of heaven?" leading out the impression that while the king was inquiring about his request and the length of time he would be gone, he was then and there talking to God about the matter.

The intense, persistent praying of Nehemiah prevailed. God can even affect the mind of a heathen ruler, and this he can do in answer to prayer without in the least overturning his free agency or forcing his will. It was a parallel case with that of Esther when she called upon her people to fast and pray for her as she went uninvited into the king's presence. As a result, his mind at a very critical moment was touched by the Spirit of God, and he was favorably moved toward Esther and held out to her the golden scepter.

Nor did the praying of Nehemiah cease when he had succeeded thus far. In building the wall of Jerusalem, he met with great opposition from Sanballat and Tobiah, who ridiculed the efforts of the people to rebuild the city's walls. Unmoved by these revilings and the intense opposition of these wicked opponents of that which was for God's cause, he pursued the task which he had undertaken. But he mixes prayer with all he does: "Hear, O our God, for we are despised; and turn their reproach upon their own head, and give them for a prey in the land of our captivity." And in continuing the account he says, "Nevertheless we made our prayer unto our God."

All along in the accounts of the high and noble work he was doing, we find prayer comes out prominently to the front. Even after the walls were completed, these same enemies of his and of the people of God again opposed him in his task. But he renews his praying, and he himself records this significant prayer: "Now there, O God, strengthen my hands."

Still further on, when Sanballat and Tobiah had hired an emissary to frighten and hinder Nehemiah, we find him setting himself directly against this new attack, and then again he turns to God in prayer: "My God, think thou upon Tobiah and Sanballat according to these their works and on the

Application to My Life:

prophetess Noadiah, and the rest of the prophets, that would have put me in fear." And God answered his faithful laborer, and defeated the counsels and the plans of these wicked opponents of Israel.

Nehemiah discovered to his dismay that the portions of the Levites had not been given them, and as a result the house of God was forsaken. He took steps to see that the lawful tithes were forthcoming so that God's house should be opened to all religious services, and appointed treasurers to give attention to this business. But prayer must not be overlooked, so we find his prayer recorded at this time: "Remember me, O my God, concerning this, and wipe not out my good deeds that I have done for the house of my God, and for the offices thereof."

Let it not be thought that this was the plea of self-righteousness as was that of the Pharisee in our Lord's time who professedly went up to the temple to pray, who paraded his self-righteous claims in God's sight. It was a prayer after the fashion of Hezekiah, who reminded God of his fidelity to Him and of his heart's being right in his sight.

Once more Nehemiah finds evil among the people of God. Just as he corrected the evil which caused the closing of the house of God, he discovers practices of Sabbath breaking, and here he has not only to counsel the people and seek to correct them by mild means, but he proposes to exercise his authority if they did not cease their buying and selling on the Sabbath Day. But he must close this part of his work also with prayer, and so he records his prayer on that occasion:

"Remember me, O my God, concerning this also, and spare me according to the greatness of thy mercy."

Lastly, as a reformer, he discovers another great evil among the people. They had intermarried with the men and women of Ashdod, Ammon and Moab. Contending with them, he caused them to reform in this matter, and the close of his record has a prayer in it:

"Remember me, O my God, because they have defiled the priesthood, and the covenant of the priesthood, and of the Levites."

Cleansing them from all strangers, he appointed the wards of the priests, and the Levites, and his recorded career closes with this brief prayer: "Remember me, O my God, for good."

Fortunate is that Church whose leaders are men of prayer. Happy is that congregation who are contemplating the erection of a church to have leaders who will lay its foundations in prayer, and whose walls go up side by side with prayer. Prayer helps to build churches and to erect the walls of houses of worship. Prayer defeats the opponents of those who are prosecut-

Application to My Life:

ing God's enterprises. Prayer touches favorably the minds even of those not connected with the Church, and moves them toward Church matters. Prayer helps mightily in all matters concerning God's cause and wonderfully aids and encourages the hearts of those who have His work in hand in this world.

Chapter 9

Samuel, The Child of Prayer

That was a grand action by Jerome, one of the Roman fathers. He laid aside all pressing engagements and went to fulfill the call God gave him, viz., to translate the Holy Scriptures. His congregations were larger than many preachers of today but he said to his people, "Now it is necessary that the Scriptures be translated; you must find you another minister: I am bound for the wilderness and shall not return until my task is finished." Away he went and labored and prayed until he produced the Latin Vulgate which will last as long as the world stands. So we must say to our friends, "I must away and have time for prayer and solitude." And though we did not write Latin Vulgates yet our work will be immortal: Glory to God.

—Rev. C. H. Spurgeon

Samuel came into this world and was given existence in direct answer to prayer. He was born of a praying mother, whose heart was full of earnest desire for a son. He came into life under prayer surroundings, and his first months in this world were spent in direct contact with a woman who knew how to pray. It was a prayer accompanied by a solemn vow that if he should be given, he should be "lent unto the Lord," and true to that vow, this praying mother put him directly in touch with the minister of the sanctuary and under the influence of "the house of prayer." It was no wonder he developed into a man of prayer. We could not have expected otherwise with such a beginning in life and with such early environments. Such surroundings always make impressions upon children and tend to make character and determine destiny.

He was in a favorable place to hear God when He spoke to him, and was in an atmosphere where it tended to his

Application to My Life:

heeding the divine call which came to him. It was the most natural thing in the world when at the third call from Heaven, when he recognized God's voice, that his childish heart responded so promptly, "Speak, Lord, thy servant heareth." Quickly was there a response from his boyish spirit, of submission, willingness and prayer.

Had he been born of a different sort of mother, had he been placed under different surroundings, had he spent his early days in contact with different influences, does any one for one moment suppose he could have easily heard the voice of God calling him to His service, and that he would have so readily yielded his young life to the God who brought him into being? Would a worldly home, with worldly surroundings, separated from the Church of God, with a worldly-minded mother, have produced such a character as Samuel? It takes such influences and agencies in early life to produce such praying men as Samuel. Would you have your child called early into divine service and separated from the world unto God? Would you have him so situated that he will be called in childhood by the Spirit of God? Put him under prayer influences. Place him near to and directly under the influence of the Man of God and in close touch with that house which is called "the house of prayer."

Samuel knew God in boyhood. As a consequence he knew God in manhood. He recognized God in childhood, obeyed him and prayed unto him. The result was that he recognized God in manhood, obeyed him, and prayed unto him. If more children were born of praying mothers, brought up in direct contact with "the house of prayer," and reared under prayer environments, more children would hear the voice of God's spirit speaking to them, and would more quickly respond to those divine calls to a religious life. Would we have praying men in our churches? We must have praying mothers to give them birth, praying homes to color their lives, and praying surroundings to impress their minds and to lay the foundations for praying lives. Praying Samuels come from praying Hannahs. Praying priests come from "the house of prayer." Praying leaders come from praying homes.

Israel for years had been under bondage to the Philistines and the ark was housed in the home of Abinadab, whose son Eleazer was appointed to keep this sacred testimony of God. The people had gone into idolatry and Samuel was disturbed about the religious condition of the nation. The ark of God was absent, the people were given to the worship of idols, and there had been a grievous departure from God. Calling upon them to put away their strange gods, he urged them to prepare their hearts unto the Lord and to begin again to serve Him—promising them that the Lord would deliver them out

Application to My Life:

of the hands of the Philistines. His preaching thus plainly to them, for with all else belonging to him, Samuel was a preacher of the times, made a deep impression and bore rich fruits as such preaching always does. "Then the children of Israel did put away Baalim and Ashtoreth, and served the Lord only."

But this was not enough. Prayer must be mixed with and must accompany their reformation So Samuel, true to his convictions about prayer, says to the people, "Gather all Israel to Mizpeh, and I will pray for you unto the Lord." While Samuel was offering up prayer for these wicked Israelites, the Philistines drew near to battle against the nation, but the Lord intervened at the critical moment and thundered with a great thunder, and discomfited these enemies of Israel, "and they were smitten before Israel."

The nation fortunately had a man who could pray, who knew the place and the worth of prayer, and a leader who had the ear of God and who could influence God.

But Samuel's praying did not stop there. He judged Israel all the days of his life, and had occasion from year to year to go in circuit to Bethel, Gilgal and Mizpeh. Then he returned home to Ramah, where he resided. "And there he built an altar unto the Lord." Here was an altar of sacrifice but as well was it an altar of prayer. And while it may have been for the benefit of the community where he lived, after the fashion of a town church, yet it must not be overlooked that it must have been a family altar, a place where the sacrifice for sin was offered but at the same time where his household gathered for worship, praise and prayer. Here Almighty God was acknowledged in the home, here was the advertisement of a religious home, and here father and mother called upon the name of the Lord, differentiating this home from all the worldly and idolatrous homes about them.

Here is an example of a religious home, the kind so greatly needed in this irreligious, godless age. Blessed is that home which has in it an altar of sacrifice and of prayer, where daily thanksgivings ascend to Heaven and where morning and night praying is done.

Samuel was not only a praying priest, a praying leader and a praying teacher and leader, but he was a praying father. And any one who knows the situation so far as family religion is concerned knows full well that the great demand of these modern times is religious homes and praying fathers and mothers. Here is where the breakdown in religion occurs, where the religious life of a community first begins to decay, and where we

Application to My Life:

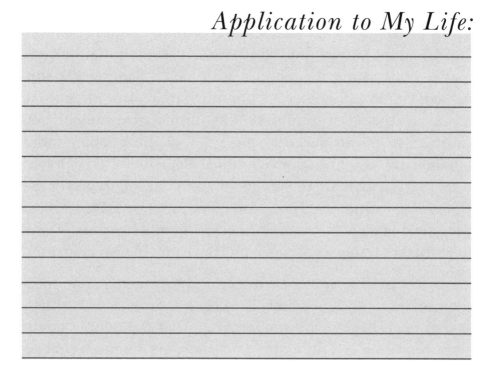

must go first to beget praying men and women in the Church of God. It is in the home that the revival must commence.

A crisis came in the history of this nation. The people were infatuated by the glory of a kingdom with a human king, and was prepared to reject God as their king, as He had always been. So they came to Samuel with the bold request, "Make us a king to judge us like all the nations." The thing displeased this man of God, who was jealous for the name, the honor and the pleasure of the Lord God. How could it be otherwise? Who would not have been likewise displeased if he were built after the pattern of Samuel? It grieved him in soul. The Lord, however, came to him just at that time with the comforting assurance so far as he was personally concerned in the transaction, that "they have not rejected thee, but they have rejected me, that I should not reign over them. Hearken unto the voice of the people, in all that they say unto thee."

Then it was that Samuel followed the bent of his mind, "And Samuel prayed unto the Lord." It seemed that in every matter concerning this people, with which Samuel was connected, he must pray over it. How much more now when there was to be an entire revolution in the form of government, and God was to be displaced as the ruler of the people, and a human king was to be set up? National affairs need to be prayed over. Praying men are demanded to carry to God in prayer the affairs of government. Lawmakers, law judges, and law executives need leaders in Israel to pray for them. How much fewer the mistakes if there was more praying done in civil matters?

But this was not to be the end of this matter. God must show so definitely and plainly His displeasure at such a request as had been made for a human king, that the people might know what a wicked thing they had done, even though God acceded to their request. They must know God still existed and had to do with this people, and with their king and the affairs of the government. So the prayers of Samuel must again be brought into play to carry out the divine purposes. So Samuel called upon the people to stand still, and he would show them what the Lord would do before their eyes. So he called upon God, and in answer God sent a tremendous storm of thunder and rain, which exceedingly terrified the people, and caused them to acknowledge their great sin in asking for a king. So afraid were the people that they hastily called upon Samuel to pray for them and to spare them from what seemed to be destruction. Samuel again prayed, and God heard and answered, and the thunder and rain ceased.

One more incident in the prayer life of Samuel is worth noticing. King Saul had been ordered to destroy all the Amalekites, root and branch, and all their stuff, but Saul, con-

Application to My Life:

trary to divine instructions, had spared King Agag and the best of the sheep and the cattle, and had justified it because he claimed that the people wanted it done.

God brought this message to Samuel at this time:

"It repenteth me that I have set up Saul to be king; for he is turned back from following me, and hath not performed my commandments."

"And it grieved Samuel, and he cried all night unto the Lord." Such a sudden declaration was enough to produce grief of soul in a man like Samuel, who loved his nation, who was true to God, and who above everything else desired the prosperity of Zion. Such grief of soul over the evils of the Church and at the sight of the abominations of the times always drives a man to his knees in prayer. Of course Samuel carried the case to God. It was a time for prayer. The case was too serious for him not to be deeply moved to pray. So greatly was the inner soul of Samuel disturbed that he prayed all night about it. Too much was at stake for him to shut his eyes to the affair, to treat it indifferently, and to let it pass without taking God into the matter, for the future welfare of Israel was in the balance.

Chapter 10

Daniel, The Praying Captive

It is a wonderful historical fact that the men of prayer have always been the men of power in the world. I want to convince you about this. Some of you men—and I am glad to see such a large number of men here tonight—if you are arguing with some friend in the workshop, be sure and ask him why it is that the men of power in the world have been the men of prayer. Take only one instance: Where did they go always to find men for the forlorn hope in Havelock's days? They went to Havelock's prayer meeting; that is where they found men who had courage to come out for the forlorn hope.

—Bishop Winnington Ingram

That was a notable experience in the life of Daniel when he was ordered by the king while in Babylon not to ask any petition of any God or king for thirty days, under penalty of being cast into the lions' den. He paid no attention to the edict, for it is recorded, "Now when Daniel knew that the writing was signed, he went into his house, and his windows being opened in his chamber toward Jerusalem, he kneeled upon his knees three times a day, and prayed and gave thanks before his God, as he did aforetime." Do not forget that this was the regular habit of this man of God. "He kneeled upon his knees and prayed as he did aforetime." What was the result? Just as expected. God sent an angel into the den of lions with Daniel and locked their mouths so that not a hair on his head was touched, and he was wonderfully delivered. Even so today deliverance always come to God's saints who tread the path of prayer as the saints of old did.

Application to My Life:

Daniel did not forget his God while in a foreign land, away from the house of God and its religious services, and deprived as he was of many religious privileges. He was a striking illustration of a young man who was decidedly religious under the most unfavorable surroundings. He proved conclusively that one could be definitely a servant of God though his environments were anything else than religious. He was among heathens so far as a God-fearing nation was concerned. There was no temple worship, no Sabbath Day, no Word of God to be read. But he had one help there which remained with him, and of which he could not be deprived, and that was his secret prayers.

Purposing in his heart without debating the question one moment or compromising at any one point, that he would not eat of the king's meat nor drink the king's wine, he stood out in that ungodly country a striking illustration of a young man, fearing God first of all, and resolving to be religious, cost what it may. But he was not to have a flowery bed on which to rest nor a smooth road on which to travel. The whimsical, tyrannical and unreasonable king, Nebuchadnezzar, was to put him to the test, and his praying qualities were to be proved. This king had a strange dream, the particular items of which passed from his memory, but the fact of the dream remained. So troubled was he about the dream, he called for all the soothsayers, astrologers and sorcerers to call the dream to mind, an impossible task, humanly speaking, and then to interpret it. He classed Daniel and his three companions, Shadrach, Meshach and Abednego, with these men, though there really was nothing in them in common with the two classes of men. Being informed that it was impossible to discover a dream like that, and at their saying if the king would tell the dream to them, they would interpret it, the king became very angry, and ordered them to be put to death. This sentence of death was against Daniel and his three companions.

But Daniel appeared upon the stage of action. At his suggestion the execution of the rash edict was held up, and he immediately called his three companions into counsel, and he urged them to unite with him in a concert of prayer that God would discover to Daniel the dream with the interpretation thereof. In answer to this united praying, it is recorded: "Then was the secret revealed unto Daniel in a night vision. Then Daniel blessed the God of heaven." As a sequel to this incident of the praying of these four men, Daniel revealed to the king his dream and its interpretation, and as a final result the king acknowledged the God of Daniel and elevated to high positions Daniel and his three associates. And it all came about because there was a praying man there just at a critical time. Blessed is that nation which has praying men who can come to the help

Application to My Life:

of civil rulers who are greatly perplexed and in great difficulties, and who can be depended upon to pray for rulers of state and Church.

Years afterward, while still in a foreign land, he still had not forgotten the God of his fathers, and to him was given the noted vision of the "Ram and the He Goat," But Daniel did not comprehend this strange vision, and yet he knew it was from God and had a deep and future meaning for nations and people. So, of course, he followed the bent of his religious mind and prayed about it.

"And it came to pass when I even I Daniel, had seen the vision, and sought for the meaning, then behold there stood before me as the appearance of a man.

"And I heard a man's voice which called, and said, Gabriel, make this man to understand the vision."

And so Gabriel made him understand the full meaning of this remarkable vision. But it came in answer to Daniel's praying. So puzzling questions may often find an answer in the closet. And as elsewhere, God employs angelic intelligences to convey information as to prayer answers. Angels have much to do with prayer. Praying men and the angels of heaven are in close touch with each other.

Some years thereafter, Daniel was studying the records of the nation, and he discovered that it was about time for the seventy years of captivity of his people to end. So he gave himself to prayer:

"And I set my face to seek by prayer and supplications, with fasting and sackcloth and ashes. And I prayed unto the Lord, and made confession."

Then follows the record in those Old Testament Scriptures of Daniel's prayer, so full of meaning, so simple in its utterances, so earnest in its spirit, so direct in its confession and requests, worthy of being patterned after.

And it was while he was speaking in prayer that the same archangel Gabriel, who seemed to have a direct interest in the praying of this man of God, "being caused to fly swiftly, touched me about the time of the evening sacrifice, and he informed me and talked with me," and then gave him much desired information valuable to Daniel.

The angels of God are much nearer us in our seasons of prayer than we imagine. God employs these glorious heavenly intelligences in the blessed work of hearing and answering prayer, when the prayer, as in the case of Daniel on this

Application to My Life:

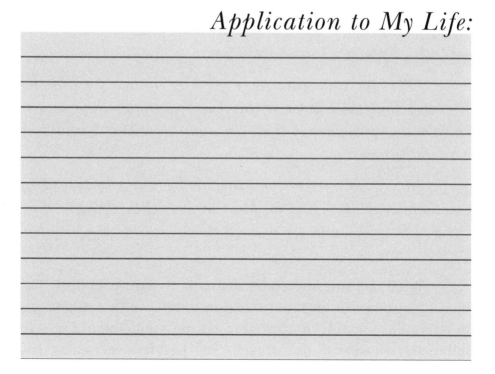

occasion, has to do with the present and future welfare of His people.

One other incident on the prayer line in the life of this captive man in Babylon. Another revelation was made to Daniel, but the time of its fulfillment appeared to be far in the future. "In those days, I Daniel was mourning three full weeks. I ate no pleasant bread, neither came flesh nor wine into my mouth till the three whole weeks were fulfilled."

It was then that he had a very strange experience and a still stranger revelation was made to him by some angelic being. It is worth while to read the scripture account:

"And behold a hand touched me, which set me on my knees, and upon the palms of my hands.

"And he said unto me, O Daniel, a man greatly beloved, understand the words that I speak unto thee, and stand upright, for unto thee am I now sent. And when he had spoken this word unto me, I stood trembling.

"Then he said unto me, Fear not, Daniel; for from the first day that thou didst set thy heart to understand and to chasten thyself before thy God, thy words were heard, and I am come for thy words.

"But the Prince of the Kingdom of Persia withstood me one and twenty days; but lo, Michael, one of the chief princes, came to help me, and I remained there with the kings of Persia."

What all this means is difficult to comprehend, but enough appears on its face to lead us to believe that the angels in heaven are deeply interested in our praying, and are sent to tell us the answers to our prayers. Further, it is very clear that some unseen forces or invisible spirits are operating to hinder the answers to our prayers. Who the Prince of Persia was who withstood this great angelic being is not divulged, but enough is revealed to know that there must be a contest in the unseen world about us between those spirits sent to minister to us in answer to our prayers and the devil and his evil spirits who seek to defeat these good spirits.

The passage furthermore gives us some intimation as to the cause of delayed answers to prayer. For "three full weeks" Daniel mourned and prayed, and for "one and twenty days" the divinely appointed angel was opposed by the "Prince of the Kingdom of Persia."

Well was it for praying Daniel that he had the courage, fortitude and determination to persist in his praying for three weeks while the fearful conflict between good and bad spirits

Application to My Life:

was going on about him unseen by mortal eyes. Well will it be for us if we do not give up in our praying when God seems not to hear and the answer is not immediate. It takes time to pray, and it takes time to get the answer to prayer. Delays in answering prayer are not denials. Failure to receive an immediate answer is no evidence that God does not hear prayer. It takes not only courage and persistence to pray successfully, but it requires much patience. "Wait on the Lord and be of good courage; and he shall strengthen thy heart; wait, I say, on the Lord."

Chapter 11

Faith of Sinners in Prayer

A certain preacher whose sermons converted many souls received a revelation from God that it was not his sermons or works by all means but the prayers of an illiterate lay brother who sat on the pulpit steps pleading for the success of the sermon. It may be in the all-revealing day so with us. We may believe after laboring long and wearily that all honor belongs to another builder whose prayers were gold, silver, and precious stones, while our sermonizings being apart from prayer are but hay and stubble.

—Rev. C. H. Spurgeon

One of the peculiar features of prayer as we study the Old Testament on this subject is the faith of unrighteous and backslidden men in prayer, and the great confidence they had in the prayers of praying men of that day. They knew certain men as men of prayer, who believed in God, who were favored of God and who prayed unto God. They recognized these men as having influence with God in averting wrath and in giving deliverance from evil.

Frequently when in trouble, when God's wrath was threatened and even when there were visitations of evil upon them for their iniquities, they showed their faith in prayer by appealing to the men who prayed, to beg God to avert His displeasure and turn aside His wrath against them. Recognizing the value of prayer as a divine agency to save men, they made application to the men who prayed, to intercede with God for them.

Application to My Life:

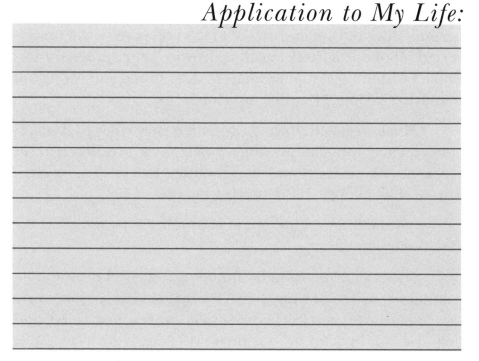

It is one of the strange paradoxes of those early days that while people departed from God, and went into grievous sin, they did not become either atheists nor unbelievers when it came to the question of the existence of a prayer-answering God. Wicked men held fast to a belief in God's existence, and to faith in the power of prayer to secure pardon for sin and to deliver them from God's wrath. It is worth something as showing the influence of the Church on sinners, when the latter believe in prayer and beg Christian people to pray for them. It is an item of interest and an event of importance when a sinner on a dying bed calls for a praying man to come to his bedside to pray for him. It means something when penitent sinners, under a sense of their guilt, feeling the displeasure of God, approach a church altar and say, "Pray for me, ye praying men and women." Little does the Church understand its full import, and still less does the Church appreciate and take in the full import of praying, especially for the unsaved men and women who ask them to pray for their immortal souls. If the Church was fully alive to God and awake to the real peril of the unconverted all about it, and was in a thriving state, more sinners would be found seeking the altars of the Church and crying out to praying people, "Pray for my soul."

Much so-called praying for sinners there may be, but it is cold, formal, official praying, which goes nowhere, never reaches God, and accomplishes nothing. Revivals begin when sinners seek the prayers of praying people.

Several things stand out in bold relief as we look at those Old Testament days:

First, the disposition of sinners against God to almost involuntarily turn to praying men for help and refuge when trouble draws near, and to invoke their prayers for relief and deliverance. "Pray for us" was their cry.

Second, the readiness with which those praying men responded to these appeals and prayed to God for those who desired this thing. Moreover, we are impressed with the fact that these praying men were always in the spirit of prayer and ready at any time to inquire of God. They were always keyed up on prayer.

Third, we note the wonderful influence these men of prayer had with God whenever they made their appeal to Him. God nearly always quickly responded and heard their praying for others. So intercessory prayer predominated in those early days of the Church.

It is a question worthy of earnest consideration, how far the present-day Church is responsible for the unbelief of sinners of these modern times in the value of prayer as an agency in averting God's wrath, in sparing barren lives and in giving

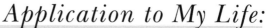

Application to My Life:

deliverance. How far is the Church responsible for the precious few mourners in Zion in these times, who ignore your altar calls and treat with indifference your appeals to come and be prayed for?

The first illustration we notice as showing the faith of wicked men in prayer and their appeal for a man of God to intercede for them is the case of the fiery serpents sent upon the Israelites. They were journeying from Mount Hor by way of the Red Sea, seeking to compass the land of Edom, when they spoke against God and Moses, after this fashion:

"Wherefore have ye brought us up out of Egypt to die in the wilderness? for there is no bread, neither is there any water; and our soul loatheth this light bread."

The thing so sorely displeased God that He sent fiery serpents among the people, and many of the people of Israel died.

"Therefore the people came to Moses, and said, We have sinned because we have spoken against the Lord, and against thee; pray unto the Lord, that He take away the serpents from us." And Moses prayed for the people.

As far as these people had departed from God, and as great as was their sin in complaining against God's dealings with them, they had not lost faith in prayer, neither did they forget that there was a leader in Israel who had influence with God in prayer, and who could by that means avert disaster and bring deliverance to them.

Jeroboam, first King of the ten tribes when the kingdom was divided, was another case in point. This was a most noted case because of the notoriety of his departure from God, which was often referred to in the after history of Israel, as "the sin of Jeroboam, the son of Nebat," and shows that despite his great wickedness in the sight of God, he did not lose his faith in the efficacy of prayer. This king on one occasion presumed to take the place of the high priest, and stood by the altar to burn incense. A man of God came out of Judah and cried against the altar and proclaimed, "Behold the altar shall be rent, and the ashes that are upon it shall be poured out." This angered Jeroboam, who saw that it was intended as a public rebuke for him, who had undertaken contrary to the Levitical law to assume the office of God's priest, and the king put forth his hand with the apparent purpose of arresting or doing violence to the man of God, saying, at the same time to those about him, "Lay hold upon him."

Immediately God smote the king with leprosy, so that he could not pull his hand back again, and at the same time the altar was rent. Astonished beyond measure at this sudden retribution for his sin, coming like lightning from Heaven, and

Application to My Life:

very much afraid, he cried out to the man of God, "Entreat now the face of the Lord thy God for me, that my hand may be restored again." And it is recorded that "the man of God besought the Lord, and the king's hand was restored him again, and became as it was before."

Let us keep in mind that we are not now considering the praying habits of the man of God nor the possibilities of prayer, though both face us here. But rather we are finding just here that a ruler in Israel, guilty of a grievous sin, and departing from God, when God's wrath falls upon him, he immediately calls upon a praying man to intercede with God in his behalf. It is but another case where a sinner against God showed his faith in the virtue of the prayers of a man of God. Sad is the day in a Christian land, not only where there is the decay of prayer in the Church, but where sinners are so unaffected by the religion of the Church that they have no faith in prayer and care little about the prayers of praying men.

Another illustration follows this case very quickly. The son of King Jeroboam fell sick, and was about to die. And this wicked, indifferent king, posted his wife off to Ahijah, the prophet of God, to ask him to say what would be the result of the illness of the child. She attempted to practice a deception upon the old prophet who was nearly blind, intending not to make herself known to him. But he had the vision of a prophet even though dim in sight, and immediately revealed to her that she was known to him. After telling her many things of vast importance concerning the kingdom and charging her husband that he had not kept God's commandments, but had gone into idolatry, he said to her: "Arise, therefore, and get thee down to thy house; and when thy feet enter into the city, the child shall die."

How natural for a father in trouble to appeal to a praying prophet for relief? And as in the first mentioned case, his sin did not blind his eyes to the value of having a man of God intercede for him. It availed nothing as was proved, but it did prove our contention that in Old Testament times sinners, while they were not themselves praying men, believed strongly in the prayers of praying men.

Take the instance of Johanan, just as the Children of Israel began their life of captivity in Babylon. Johanan and Jeremiah, with a small company, had been left in their native land, and Ishmael had conspired against Gedaliah, the appointed governor of the country, and had slain him. Johanan came to the rescue and delivered the people from Ishmael who was taking them away from their land. But Johanan wanted to flee down into Egypt, which was contrary to the Divine plan. At this

Application to My Life:

particular juncture of affairs, he assembled all the people, and they went to Jeremiah with the earnest appeal:

"We beseech thee, let our supplication be accepted before thee, and pray for us unto the Lord thy God, that the Lord thy God may show us the way wherein we may walk, and the thing that we may do."

Like all other appeals to good men for prayer, Jeremiah interceded for these inquirers after the right way, and after ten days the answer came, and they were informed by Jeremiah what God would have them do. This was to the effect that they should not go down to Egypt, but remain in and about Jerusalem, but the people and Johanan played Jeremiah false, and refused to do as God had told them in answer to prayer. But it did not disprove the fact that they had faith in prayer and in praying men.

Another case may be noticed as showing the truth of our proposition that sinners had faith in prayer in the Old Testament dispensation, thus indirectly proving the preeminence of prayer in those days, for certainly prayer must have had a prominent place and its necessity must have received general recognition, when even sinners by their actions give endorsement to its virtue and necessity. Surely if sinners bore testimony to its worth, and at that time displayed their need of prayer, even by the prayers of some one else, Church people of this day ought to have a deep sense of its need, and should have strong faith in prayer and its virtue. And certainly if the men of Old Testament times were such men of prayer, and had such a reputation as praying men, then in this favored day, Christian men should be so given to prayer that they also would have a wide reputation as praying men.

Zedekiah was king of Judah just as the captivity of God's people began. He was in charge of the kingdom when Jerusalem was besieged by the King of Babylon. And it was just about this time that Zedekiah sent two chosen men unto Jeremiah saying: "Inquire, I pray thee, of the Lord for us; for Nebuchadnezzar, king of Babylon, maketh war against us; if so be that the Lord will deal with us according to all his wondrous works, that he may go up from us."

And God told Jeremiah in answer to this inquiry what to do, and what would occur, but as in another case, that of Johanan, Zedekiah proved false, and would not do as God instructed Jeremiah to tell him. At the same time it proved conclusively that Zedekiah had not lost his faith in prayer as a means of finding out the mind of God, nor did it affect him in his belief in the virtue of the prayers of a praying man.

Application to My Life:

Verily, prayer must have had a preeminent place in all Old Testament history when not only the men of God were noted for their praying habits, but even men who departed from God and proved false bore testimony to its virtue by appealing to the men of prayer to make intercessions for them. This is so notorious in Old Testament history that no careful reader of these old scriptures can fail to discover and notice it.

Chapter 12

Paul, The Teacher of Prayer

Fletcher of Madeley, a great teacher of a century and a half ago, used to lecture to the young theological students. He was one of the fellow-workers with Wesley and a man of most saintly character. When he had lectured on one of the great topics of the Word of God, such as the Fullness of God's Holy Spirit or on the power and blessing that He meant His people to have, he would close the lecture and say, "That is the theory; now will those who want the practice come along up to my room!" And again and again they closed their books and went away to his room, where the hour's theory would be followed by one or two hours of prayer.

—*Rev. Hubert Brooke*

How instant, strenuous, persistent, and pathetic was Paul's urgency of prayer upon those to whom he wrote and spoke! "I exhort," says he, writing to Timothy, "first of all, that supplications, prayers, intercessions and giving of thanks be made for all men." This he meant was to be the prime deposit and truth for the Church. First of all, before all things, to the front of all things, the Church of Christ was to be a praying Church, was to pray for men, was to pray for all men. He charged the Philippians to this effect: "Be careful for nothing, but in everything, by prayer and supplication, with thanksgiving, let your requests be made known unto God." The Church must be anxious about nothing. In everything prayer must be made. Nothing was too small about which to pray. Nothing was too great for God to overcome.

Paul lays it down as a vital, all-essential injunction in writing to the Church at Thessalonica, "Rejoice evermore. Pray

Application to My Life:

without ceasing. In everything give thanks. For this is the will of God concerning you." The Church must give itself to unceasing prayer. Never was prayer to cease in the Church. This was the will of God concerning His Church on earth.

Paul was not only given to prayer himself, but he continually and earnestly urged it in a way that showed its vital importance. He was not only insistent in urging prayer upon the Church in his day, but he urged persistent praying. "Continue in prayer and watch in the same," was the keynote of all his exhortations on prayer. "Praying always with all prayer and supplication," was the way he pressed this important matter upon the people. "I will, therefore," I exhort, this is my desire, my mind upon this question, "that men pray everywhere, without wrath and doubting." As he prayed after this fashion himself, he could afford to press it upon those to whom he ministered.

Paul was a leader by appointment and by universal recognition and acceptance. He had many mighty forces in this ministry. His conversion, so conspicuous and radical, was a great force, a perfect magazine of aggressive and defensive warfare. His call to the apostleship was clear, luminous and convincing. But these forces were not the divinest energies which brought forth the largest results to his ministry. Paul's course was more distinctly shaped and his career rendered more powerfully successful by prayer than by any other force.

It is no surprise then that he should give such prominence to prayer in his preaching and writing. We could not expect it to be otherwise. As prayer was the highest exercise in his personal life, so also prayer assumed the same high place in his teaching. His example of prayer added force to his teaching on prayer. His practice and his teaching ran in parallel lines. There was no inconsistency in the two things.

Paul was the chiefest of the apostles as he was chief in prayer. If he was the first of the apostles, prayer conspired to that end. Hence he was all the better qualified to be a teacher on prayer. His praying fitted him to teach others what prayer was and what prayer could do. And for this reason he was competent to urge upon the people that they must not neglect prayer. Too much depended upon it.

He was first in prayer for this cause. For the reason that on him centered more saintly praying than on any one else, he became the first in apostleship. The crown of martyrdom was the highest crown in the royalty of Heaven, but prayer put this crown of martyrdom on his head.

He who would teach the people to pray must first himself be given to prayer. He who urges prayer on others must first tread the path of prayer himself. And just in proportion as

Application to My Life:

preachers pray, will they be disposed to urge prayer upon those to whom they preach. Moreover, just in proportion as preachers pray, will they be fitted to preach on prayer. If that course of reasoning be true, would it be legitimate to draw the conclusion that the reason why there is so little preaching on prayer in these modern times is because preachers are not praying men?

We might stake the whole question of the absolute necessity and the possibilities of prayer in this dispensation on Paul's attitude toward prayer. If personal force, if the energy of a strong will, if profound convictions, if personal culture and talents, and if the Divine call and the Divine empowerment,— if any one of these, or all of them united, could direct the Church of God without prayer, then logically prayer would be unnecessary. If profound piety and unswerving consecration to a high purpose, if impassioned loyalty to Jesus Christ, if any or all of these could exist without devoted prayer, or lift a Church leader above the necessity of prayer, then Paul was above its use. But if the great and gifted, the favored and devoted Paul felt the necessity of unceasing prayer, and realized that it was urgent and pressing in regard to its claims and necessity, and if he felt that it was clamorous and insistent that the Church should pray without ceasing, then he and his brethren in the apostolate should be aided by universal and mighty praying.

Paul's praying and his commands and the urgency with which he pressed upon the Church to pray, is the most convincing proof of the absolute necessity of prayer as a great moral force in the world, an indispensable and inalienable factor in the progress and spread of the Gospel, and in the development of personal piety. In Paul's view, there was no Church success without prayer, and no piety without prayer, in fact without much prayer. A Church out of whose life streams prayer as the incense flames went out of the censer, and a leadership out of whose character, life and habits flames prayer as imposing, conspicuous and spontaneous as the fragrant incense flamed, this was the leadership for God.

To pray everywhere, to pray in everything, to continue instant in prayer, and to pray without ceasing, thus Paul spoke as a commentator on the Divine uses and the nature of prayer.

Timothy was very dear to Paul, and the attachment was mutual and intensified by all their affinities. Paul found in Timothy those elements which fitted him to be his spiritual successor, at least the depository and the leader of the great spiritual principles and forces which were essential to the establishment and prosperity of the Church. These primary and vital truths he would enforce on and radicate in Timothy. Paul regarded Timothy as one to whom fundamental and vital truths might

Application to My Life:

be committed, who would preserve them truly, and who would commit them inviolate to the future. So he gives to Timothy this deposit of prayer for all ages as found in 1 Tim. 2:1.

Let it be noted before we go any further that Paul wrote directly under the superintendency of the Holy Spirit, who guarded Paul against error, and who suggested the truths which Paul taught. We hold definitely without compromise in the least to the plenary inspiration of the Scriptures, and as Paul's writings are part and parcel of those Sacred Writings, then Paul's Epistles are portions of the Scriptures or the Word of God. This being true, the doctrine of prayer which Paul affirmed is the doctrine of the Holy Spirit. His Epistles are of the Word of God, inspired, authentic and of Divine authority. So that prayer as taught by Paul is the doctrine which Almighty God would have His Church accept, believe, and practice.

These words to Timothy, therefore, were divinely inspired words. This section of Holy Writ is much more than merely suggestive, and is far more than a broad, bare outline on prayer. It is so instructive about prayer, about how men ought to pray, how business men should pray, and so forceful about the reasons why men ought to pray, that it needs to be strongly and insistently pressed.

Here are Paul's words to Timothy on prayer:

"I exhort, therefore, that, first of all, supplications, prayers, intercessions and giving of thanks, be made for all men;

"For kings and all that are in authority that we may lead a quiet and peaceable life in all godliness and honesty.

"For this is good and acceptable in the sight of God, our Saviour;

"Who will have all men to be saved and to come to the knowledge of the truth.

"For there is one God, and one Mediator between God and men, the man Christ Jesus;

"Who gave himself a ransom for all, to be testified in due time. I will therefore that men pray everywhere, lifting up holy hands, without wrath and doubting."

In this prayer section we have set forth by Paul the inheritance and practice of every Christian in all ages. It is a vade mecum in the great business of praying. it gives us a view of the energy and many-sidedness of prayer. First in point of time in all excellence of all duties is prayer. It must be first in all occupations. So exacting and imperative in its import and power is prayer that it stands first among spiritual values. He that prays not, is not at all. He is naught, less than naught. He is below

Application to My Life:

zero, so far as Christ and God and heaven are concerned. Not simply among the first things does prayer stand on a level with other things, but first of the first, to the very forefront, does Paul put prayer with all his heart. "I exhort that first of all."

His teaching is that praying is the most important of all things on earth. All else must be restrained, retired, to give it primacy. Put it first, and keep its primacy. The conflict is about the primacy of prayer. Defeat and victory lie in this one thing. To make prayer secondary is to discrown it. It is to fetter and destroy prayer. If prayer is put first, then God is put first, and victory is assured. Prayer must either reign in the life or must abdicate. Which shall it be?

According to Paul, "supplications, prayers, intercessions and giving of thanks" all these elements of prayer and forms of prayer are to be offered for men. Prayer is offered for things, for all things, for all temporal good, and for all spiritual good and grace, but in these directions Paul rises to the highest results and purposes of prayer. Men are to be affected by prayer. Their good, their character, conduct and destiny are all involved in prayer. In this regard prayer moves along the highest way, and pursues its loftiest end. We are cognizant and consonant with things, with blessings, and bestowments, with matters and things which touch men, but men themselves are here set forth as the objects of prayer. This broadens and ennobles prayer. Men, through the whole sweep and range of their conditions, are to be held in the mighty grasp of prayer.

Paul's teaching is to the effect that prayer is essentially a thing of the inner nature. The spirit within us prays. So note Paul's directions: "I will therefore that men pray everywhere, without wrath." "Wrath" is a term which denotes the natural, internal motion of plants and fruits, swelling with juice. The natural juices are warmed into life, and rise by the warmth of

Spring. Man has in him natural juices which rise as does the sap. Warmth, heat, all stages of passions and desires, every degree of feeling, these spontaneously rise under provocation. Guard against and suppress them. Man cannot pray with these natural feelings rising in him, cultivated, cherished and continued there. Prayer is to be without these. "Without wrath." Higher, better, nobler inspiration are to lift prayer upward. "Wrath" depresses prayer, hinders it, suppresses it.

The word "without" means making no use of, having no association with, apart from, aloof from. The natural, unrenewed heart has no part in praying. Its heat and all its nature juices poison and destroy praying. The nature of prayer is deeper than nature. We cannot pray by nature, even by the kindliest and the best nature.Prayer is the true test of character. Fidelity to our conditions and trueness to our relations are often evinced by our prayerfulness. Some conditions give birth

Application to My Life:

to prayer. They are the soil which germinates and perfects prayer. To pray under some circumstances seems very fitting. Not to pray in some conditions seems heartless and discordant. The great storms of life, when we are helpless and without relief, or are devoid of assuagement, are the natural and providential conditions of prayer.

Widowhood is a great sorrow. It comes to saintly women as well as to others. True widows there are who are saintly. They are to be honored and their sorrow is divine. Their piety is aromatic and lightened by their bruised hearts. Here is Paul's description of such widows:

"Now she that is a widow indeed and desolate, trusteth in God, and continueth in supplications and prayers night and day. But she that liveth in pleasure is dead while she liveth."

Here is the striking contrast between two classes of women. One gives herself to supplications night and day. The other lives in pleasure and is spiritually dead. So Paul describes a true widow as being great in prayer. Her prayers, born of her faith and desolation, are a mighty force. Day and night her prayers go up to God unceasingly. The widowhood heart is a mighty appeal to God when that heart is found in the way of prayer, intense, unwearied prayer.

One of Paul's striking injunctions worthy of study is this one, "continuing instant in prayer," or as the Revised Version reads, "Continuing steadfast in prayer," which is his description of prayer. The term means to tarry, to remain, to be steadfast and faithful in prayer, to stick to it strong, to stay at it with strength to the end, to give attention to it with vigor, devotion and constancy, to give unremitting care to it.

Praying is a business, a life-long business, one to be followed with diligence, fervor and toil. The Christian's business by way of preeminence is prayer. It is his most engaging, most heavenly, most lucrative business. Prayer is a business of such high and deserved dignity and import that it is to be followed "without ceasing." That is, with no let up nor break down, followed assiduously and without intermission. To prayer we are to give all strength. It must cover all things, be in every place, find itself in all seasons, and embrace everything, always, and everywhere.

In the remarkable prayer in Ephes. 3, he is praying for wide reaches of religious experience. He is there bowing his knees unto God, in the name of Jesus Christ, and asking that God would grant that these Ephesian believers would in their experiences go far beyond the utmost stretches of past sainthood. "Filled with all the fullness of God," an experience so great and so glorious that it makes the head of the modern saint so dizzy that he is afraid to look up to those supernal heights or

Application to My Life:

peer down into the fathomless depths. Paul just passes us on to Him, "who is able to do exceeding abundantly above all that we can ask or think." This is a specimen of his teaching on prayer.

In writing to the Philippian Church, Paul recounts the situation, and shows the transmuting power of prayer as follows:

"Some indeed preach Christ of envy and strife; and some also of good will;

"The one preach Christ of contention, not sincerely, supposing to add affliction to my bonds;

"But the other of love, knowing that I am set for the defense of the Gospel.

"What then? Notwithstanding every way, whether in pretense or in truth, Christ is preached; and I therein do rejoice, yea, and will rejoice.

"For I know that this shall turn to my salvation through our prayer and the supply of the Spirit of Jesus Christ.

"According to my earnest expectation and my hope; that in nothing shall I be ashamed, but that with all boldness, as always, so now also Christ shall be magnified in my body, whether it be by life or death."

Boldness was to be secured by him and discomfiture and shame prevented by their prayers, and Christ was to be gloriously magnified by and through Paul, whether he lived or died.

It is to be remarked that in all these quotations in Corinthians, Ephesians or Philippians, the Revised Version gives us the most intense form of prayer, "supplications." It is the intense, personal, strenuous, persistent praying of the saints, that Paul requests, and they must give special strength, interest, time and heart to their praying to make it bear its largest golden fruit.

The general direction about prayer to the Colossian Christians is made specific and is sharpened to the point of a personal appeal: "Continue in prayer and watch in the same, with thanksgiving; withal praying also for us, that God would open unto us a door of utterance, to speak the mystery of Christ, for which I am also in bonds; that I make it manifest as I ought to speak."

Paul is accredited with the authorship of the Epistle to the Hebrews. We have it in a reference to the character of Christ's praying, which is illustrative, directory and authentative as to the elements of true praying. How deep tones are his words! How heart-affecting and how sublime was His praying who prayed as never man prayed before, and yet prayed in

Application to My Life:

order to teach man how to pray, "who in the days of His flesh, when He had offered prayers and supplications, with strong crying and tears, to Him that was able to save Him from death, and was heard in that He feared." The praying of Jesus Christ drew on the mightiest forces of His being. His prayers were His sacrifices, which He offered before He offered Himself on the cross for the sins of mankind. Prayer-sacrifice is the forerunner and pledge of self-sacrifice. We must die in our closets before we can die on the cross.

Chapter 13

Paul and His Praying

In the life of Frank Crossley it is told how one day in 1888 he had said good-bye at the station to his friends, General and Mrs. Booth; but before they steamed out he handed a letter to them giving details of a sacrifice he had resolved to make for the Army. He came home and was praying alone. "As I was praying," he said, "there came over me the most extraordinary sense of joy. It was not exactly in my head, nor in my heart, it was almost a grasping of my chest by some strange hand that filled me with an ecstasy I never had before. It was borne in on me that this was the joy of the Lord." So this servant of God made in his pilgrimage to God an advance from which he never fell back. He thought it likely at the time that the Booths had read this letter in the train and this was an answer to prayer of theirs; afterwards he heard they had prayed for him in the train just after getting wess out of Manchester.

— Rev. Edward Shillito

He who studies Paul's praying, both his prayers and his commands about prayer, will find what a wide, general, minute, and diversified area it covers. It will appear that these men like Wesley, Brainerd, Luther, and all their holy successors in the spiritual realms, were not guilty of fanaticism nor superstition when they ordered all things by prayer great and small, and committed all things, secular and religious, natural and spiritual, to God in prayer. In this they were but following the great exemplar and authority of the Apostle Paul.

To seek God as Paul did by prayer, to commune with God as Paul did, to supplicate Jesus Christ as Paul did, to seek the Holy Spirit by prayer as Paul did, to do this without ceasing, to be always a racer, and to win Christ as Paul did by prayer—all this makes a saint, an apostle, and a leader for God. This kind of a life engages, absorbs, enriches, and empowers with God and for God. Prayer, if successful, must always engage and

Application to My Life:

absorb us. This kind of praying brings Pauline days and secures Pauline gifts. Pauline days are good, Pauline gifts are better, but Pauline praying is best of all, for it brings Pauline days and secures Pauline gifts. Pauline praying is worth all it costs. Prayer which costs nothing gets nothing. It is beggarly business at best.

Paul's estimate of prayer is seen and enforced by the fact that Paul was a man of prayer. His high position in the Church was not one of dignity and position to enjoy and luxuriate in. It was not one of officialism, nor was it one of arduous and exhaustless toil, for Paul was preeminently a praying man.

He began his great career for Christ in the great struggle and school of prayer. God's convincing and wonderful argument to assure Ananias was, "Behold he prayeth." Thee days was he without sight, neither eating nor drinking, but the lesson was learned well.

He went out on his first great missionary trip under the power of fasting and prayer, and they, Paul and Barnabas, established every Church by the very same means, by fasting and prayer. He began his work in Philippi "where prayer was wont to be made." As "they went to prayer," the spirit of divination was cast out of the young woman. And when Paul and Silas were put in prison, at midnight they prayed and sang praises to God.

Paul made praying a habit, a business and a life. He literally gave himself to prayer. So with him praying was not an outer garb, a mere coloring, a paint, a polish. Praying made up the substance, the bone, the marrow, and the very being of his religious life. His conversion was a marvel of grace and power. His apostolic commission was full and royal. But he did not vainly expect to make full proof of his ministry, by the marvels of conditions and by wonderful results in the conversion, nor by the apostolic commission signed and sealed by Divine authority, and carrying with it all highest gifts and apostolic enrichments, but by prayer, by ceaseless, wrestling, agonizing and Holy Spirit praying. Thus did Paul work his wrok, and crown his work, his life and the death with martyr principles and with martyr glory.

Paul had a spiritual trait which was very marked and especially promised, and it was that of prayer. He had a profound conviction that prayer was a great as well as a solemn duty; that prayer was a royal privilege; that prayer was a mighty force; that prayer gauges piety, makes faith mighty and mightier; that much prayer was necessary to Christian success; that prayer was a great factor in the ongoing of God's kingdom on earth; and that God and heaven expected to pray.

Somehow we are dependent on prayer for great triumphs of holiness over sin, of heaven over hell, and of Christ

Application to My Life:

over satan. Paul took it for granted that men who know God would pray; that men who lived for God would pray much, and that men could not live for God who did not pray. So Paul prayed much. He was in the habit of praying. He was used to praying, and that formed the habit of prayer. He estimated prayer so greatly that he fully knew its value, and that fastened the habit on him. Paul was in the habit of praying because he loved God, and such love in the heart always finds its expression in regular habits of prayer. He felt the need of much grace, and of more and more grace, and grace only comes through the channels of prayer, and only abounds more and more as prayer abounds more and more.

Paul was in the habit of praying, but he prayed not by mere force of habit. Man is such a creature of habit that he is always in danger of doing things simply by heart, in a routine, prefunctory manner. Paul's habit was regular and hearty. To the Romans he writes, "For God is my witness, that without ceasing, I make mention of you always in my prayers." Prison doors are opened and earthquakes take place by such praying as Paul did, even by such melodious Pauline praying. All things are opened to the kind of praying which was done by Paul and Silas. All things are opened by prayer. They could shut up Paul from preaching, but this could not shut him up from praying. And the Gospel could win its way by Paul's praying as well as by Paul's preaching. The apostle might be in prison, but the Word of God was free, and went like the mountain air, while the apostle is bound in prison and abounds in prayer.

How profound their joy in Jesus which expressed itself so happily and so sweetly in praise and prayer, under conditions so painful and so depressing! Prayer brought them into full communion with God which made all things radiant with the Divine presence which enabled them to "rejoice that they were counted worthy to suffer shame for His name, and to count it all joy when they fell into divers trials." Prayer sweetens all things and sanctifies all things. The prayerful saint will be a suffering saint. Suffering prayerfully he will be a sweet saint. A praying saint will be a praising saint. Praise is but prayer set to music and song.

After that notable charge to the elders at Ephesus, as he tarried there while on his way to Jerusalem, this characteristic record is made in Acts:

"And when he had thus spoken, he kneeled down and prayed with them. And they all wept sore, and fell on Paul's neck and kissed him."

"He kneeled down and prayed." Note those words. Kneeling in prayer was Paul's favorite attitude, the fitting posture of an earnest, humble suppliant. Humility and intensity

Application to My Life:

are in such a position in prayer before Almighty God. It is the proper attitude of man before God, of a sinner before a Saviour, and of a beggar before his benefactor. To seal his sacred and living charge to those Ephesian elders by praying was that which made the charge efficient, benignant and abiding.

Paul's religion was born in the throes of that three days' struggle of prayer, while he was in the house of Ananias, and there he received a divine impetus which never slackened till it brought him to the gates of the eternal city. That spiritual history and religious experience projected along the line of unceasing prayer, brought him to the highest spiritual altitudes and yields the largest spiritual results. Paul lived in the very atmosphere of prayer. His first missionary trip was projected by prayer. It was by prayer and fasting that he was called into the foreign missionary field, and by the same means the Church at Antioch was moved to send forth Paul and Barnabas on their first missionary journey. Here is the Scripture record of it:

"Now there were in the Church which was at Antioch certain prophets and teachers, as Barnabas and Simeon, that was called Niger; and Lucius of Cyrene, and Manean, which had been brought up with Herod the tetrach, and Saul.

"And as they ministered to the Lord, and fasted, the Holy Ghost said, Separate me Barnabas and Saul for the work whereunto I have called them.

"And when they had fasted and prayed, and had laid their hands on them, they sent them away."

Here is a model for all missionary outgoings, a presage of success. Here was the Holy Spirit directing a prayerful Church obedient to the Divine leadership, and this condition of things brought forth the very largest possible results in the mission of these two men of God. We may confidently assert that no

Church in which Paul was prominent would be a prayerless Church. Paul lived, toiled and suffered in an atmosphere of prayer. To him, prayer was the very heart and life of religion, its bone and marrow, the motor of the Gospel, and the sign by which it conquered. We are not left in ignorance, for that spirit established churches, putting in them the everlasting requisite of self-denial, in the shape of fasting, and in the practice of prayer. Here is the Divine record of Paul's work on this line:

"Confirming the souls of the disciples, and exhorting them to continue in the faith, and that we must through much tribulation enter into the kingdom of God.

"And when they had ordained them elders in every Church, and had prayed with fasting, they commended them to the Lord, on whom they believed."

Application to My Life:

In obedience to a heavenly vision, Paul lands in Europe, and finds himself at Philippi. There is no synagogue, and few if any Jews are there. A few pious women, however, have a meeting place for prayer, and Paul is drawn by spiritual attraction and spiritual affinities to the place "where prayer is wont to be made." And Paul's first planting of the Gospel in Europe is at that little prayer meeting. He is there the chief pray-er and the leading talker. Lydia was the first convert at that prayer meeting. They protracted the meeting. They called it a meeting for prayer.

It was while they were going to that protracted prayer meeting that Paul performed the miracle of casting the devil of divination out of a poor demon-possessed girl, who had been made a source of gain by some covetous men, the results of which, by the magistrate's orders, were his scourging and imprisonment. The result by God's orders was the conversion of the jailer and his whole household. To the praying apostle no discouragements are allowed. A few praying women are enough for an apostolical field of labor.

In this last incident we have a picture of Paul at midnight. He is in the inner prison, dark and deadly. He has been severely and painfully scourged, his clothing is covered with blood, while there are blood clots on his gnashed and torn body. His feet are in the stocks, every nerve is feverish and swollen, sensitive and painful. But we find him under these very unfavorable and suffering conditions at his favorite pursuit. Paul is praying with Silas, his companion, in a joyous, triumphant strain. "And at midnight, Paul and Silas prayed and sang praises unto God, and the prisoners heard them. And suddenly there was an earthquake, so that the foundation of the prison was shaken, and immediately all the doors were shaken; and every one's ban was loosed. And the keeper of the prison awaking out of his sleep, and seeing the prison doors opened, he drew out his sword, and would have killed himself, supposing that the prisoners had been fled.

"But Paul cried out with a loud voice saying, Do thyself no harm; for we are all here."

Never was prayer so beautiful, never more resultful. Paul was an adept at prayer, a lover of prayer, a wondrous devotee of prayer, who could pursue it with such joyous strains, under such conditions of despondency and despair. What a mighty weapon of defense was prayer to Paul! How songful! The angels doubtless stilled their highest and sweetest notes to listen to the music which bore those prayers to heaven. The earthquake trod along the path made by the mighty forces of Paul's praying. He did not go out when his chains were loosed, and the stocks fell off. His praying taught him that God had nobler purposes that

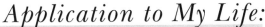

Application to My Life:

night than his own individual freedom. His praying and the earthquake alarm were to bring salvation to that prison, freedom from the thraldom and prison house of sin which was prefigured to him by his body emancipation. God's mighty providence had opened his prison door and had broken his prison bonds, not to give freedom, but to give freedom to the jailer. God's providential openings are often to test our ability to stay rather than to go. It tested Paul's ability to stay.

Chapter 14

Paul and His Praying (Continued)

William Law has this very pertinent word in his "Devout Life": "When you begin your petitions use such various expressions of the attributes of God as may make you most sensible of the greatness and power of the Divine nature?" And then William Law gives various examples, which I am bound to say would not be helpful to me, as they would imprison my spirit in a coat of mail. But I want to emphasize and commend the principle of it, which is, that our fellowship should begin with the primary elements of adoration and praise.

—Rev. J. H. Jowett

There are two occasions with wonderful results where the statement is not explicit that Paul was in prayer, but the circumstances and the results, and Paul's universal and intense praying habit, make it most evident that the key to the results of both occasions is prayer. The first occasion is when Paul sailed away from Philippi and came to Troas, where he abode seven days. On the first day of the week, when the disciples came together to break bread, Paul preached unto them, expecting to depart on the morrow, and continued his preaching till late in the night.

There was sitting in the window a young man named Eutychus, who naturally fell asleep, and as Paul was rather long in speaking, the young man fell out of the high window, and was taken up for dead. Paul went down to the place where the young man had fallen, and embracing him, told the people about him that they need not be troubled, for life was still in the

Application to My Life:

body. Paul returned to the upper room, where he had been preaching, and talked with the disciples till break of day. And the young man was brought alive, and as a consequence all were greatly comforted.

The very natural conclusion without the fact being specially stated is that Paul must have prayed for the young man when he embraced him, and his prayer was answered in the quick recovery of the young man.

The second occasion was in the perilous and protracted storm which overtook the vessel in which Paul was being carried as a prisoner to Rome. They were being exceedingly tossed about with the great tempest, and neither sun nor stars appeared as they were beset and struggled against wind and storm. All hope that they would be saved seemed gone. But after long abstinence, Paul stood in the midst of those on board, and speaking more particularly to the officers of the vessel, said, "Sirs, ye should have hearkened unto me, and not have loosed from Crete, and to have gained this harm and loss. And now I exhort you, to be of good cheer, for there shall be no loss of any man's life among you, but of the ship. For there stood by this night the angel of God, whose I am and whom I serve, saying, Fear not, Paul; thou must be brought before Caesar, and lo, God hath given thee all them that sail with thee. Wherefore, sirs, be of good cheer; for I believe God, that it shall be even as God hath told me."

It requires no strained interpretation to read into this simple record the fact that Paul must have been praying when the angel appeared unto him with that message of encouragement and assurance of safety. Paul's habit of prayer and his strong belief in prayer must have driven him to his knees. Such an emergency with him would necessarily move him to pray under such crucial circumstances.

After the shipwreck, while on the island of Melita, we have another representation of Paul at prayer. He is at his work of praying for a very ill man. While a fire was being made, a deadly poisonous viper fastened itself on his hand, and the barbarians immediately concluded it was a case of retribution for some crime Paul had committed, but they soon discovered that Paul did not die, and changed their minds and concluded that he was a sort of god.

In the same quarter at the time, was the father of Publius, who was very ill of a fever, and bloody flux, approaching seemingly his end. Paul went to him, and laid his hands upon him, and with simple confidence in God he prayed, and immediately the disease was rebuked, and the man was healed. When the natives of the island beheld this remarkable incident, they brought others to Paul, and they were healed, after the same fashion, by Paul's praying.

Application to My Life:

Turning back in Paul's life to the time he was at Ephesus on his way to Jerusalem, we find him stopping at Tyre after he departed from Ephesus. Before leaving Ephesus he had prayed with them all. But he did not trust in his words howsoever strong, fitting and solemn they might have been. God must be recognized, invoked and sought. Paul did not take it for granted, after he had done his best, that God as a master of course would bless his efforts to do good, but he sought God. God does not do things in a matter-of-course sort of way. God must be invoked, sought unto, and put into things by prayer.

Following his visit to Ephesus, he arrived at Tyre, where he stopped a few days. Here he found some disciples, who begged Paul not to go to Jerusalem, saying through the Spirit that he should not go up to that city. But Paul adhered to his original purpose to go to Jerusalem. The account says:

"And when we had accomplished those days, we departed, and went our way; and they all brought us on our way with their wives and children, till we were out of the city; and we kneeled down on the shore and prayed."

What a sight to behold on that seashore! Here is a family picture of love and devotion, where husbands, wives and even children are present, and prayer is made out in the open air. What an impression it must have made upon those children! The vessel was ready to depart, but prayer must cement their affections and sanctify wives and children, and bless their parting—a parting which was to be final so far as this world was concerned. The scene is beautiful and does honor to the head and heart of Paul, to his person and his piety, and shows the tender affection in which he was held. His devoted habit of sanctifying all things by prayer comes directly to the light. "We kneeled down on the shore and prayed." Never did sea strand see a grander picture or witness a lovelier sight—Paul on his knees on the sands of that shore, invoking God's blessing upon these men, women and children.

When Paul was arraigned at Jerusalem, in making his public defense, he refers to two instances of his praying. One was when he was in the house of Judas, in Damascus, after he had been stricken to the earth and brought under conviction. He was there three days, and to him was Ananias sent, to lay his hand upon him, at the time of his blindness and darkness. It was during those three days of prayer. This is the Scriptural record, and the words are those of Ananias addressed to him:

"And now why tarriest thou? Arise and be baptized, and wash away thy sins, calling on the name of the Lord."

The Lord had emboldened the timid Ananias to go and minister to Paul, by telling him, "Behold he prayeth." And so we have in this reference Paul's prayerfulness intensified by

Application to My Life:

the exhortation of Ananias. Prayer precedes pardon of sins. Prayer becomes those who seek God. Prayer belongs to the earnest, sincere inquirer after God. Pardon of sin and acceptance with God always come at the end of earnest praying. The evidence of sincerity in a true seeker of religion isthat it can be said of him, "Behold he prayeth."

The other reference in his defense lets us into the prayerful intenseness into which his whole religious life had been fashioned and shows us how in the absorbing ecstasy of prayer, the vision came and directions were received by which his toilsome life was to be guided. Also we see the familiar terms on which he stood and talked with his Lord:

"And it came to pass when I was come again to Jerusalem, even while I prayed in the temple, I was in a trance;

"And saw him saying unto me, Make haste and get thee quickly out of Jerusalem, for they will not receive thy testimony concerning me.

"And I said, Lord, they know that I imprisoned and beat in every synagogue them that believed on thee.

"And when the blood of thy martyr Stephen was shed, I also was standing by, and consenting to his death, and kept the raiment of them that slew him.

"And he said unto me, Depart, for I will send thee far hence unto the Gentiles."

Prayer always brings directions from heaven as to what God would have us to do. If we prayed more and more directly, we should make fewer mistakes in life as to duty. God's will concerning us is revealed in answer to prayer. If we prayed more and prayed better and sweeter, then clearer and more entrancing visions would be given us, and our intercourse with God, would be of the most intimate, free, and bold order.

It is difficult to itemize or classify Paul's praying. It is so comprehensive, so discursive, and so minute, that it is no easy task to do so. Paul teaches much about prayer in his didactics. He specifically enforces the duty and necessity of prayer upon the Church, but that which was better for Paul and better for us is that he himself prayed much and illustrated his own teaching. He practiced what he preached. He put to the test the exercise of prayer which he urged upon the people of his day.

To the Church at Rome he plainly and specifically asseverated with solemnity his habit of praying. This he wrote to those Roman believers:

Application to My Life:

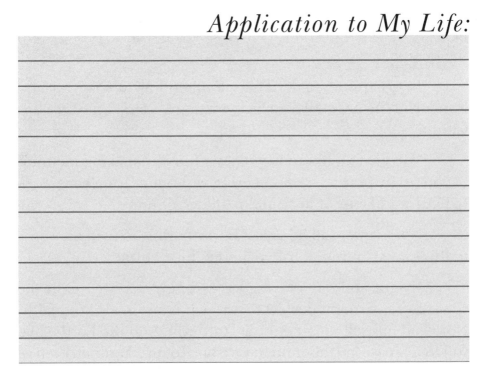

For God is my witness, whom I serve with my spirit in the Gospel of His Son, that without ceasing I make mention of you always in my prayers."

Paul not only prayed for himself. He made a practice of praying for others. He was preeminently an intercessor. As he urged intercessory prayer on others, so he interceded himself for others beside himself.

He begins that remarkable Epistle to the Romans in the spirit of prayer: He closes it with this solemn charge: "Now I beseech you, brethren, for the Lord Jesus Christ's sake, and for the love of the Spirit, that ye strive with me in your prayers to God for me."

But this is not all. In the very heart of that Epistle, he commands "Continuing instant in prayer." That is, give constant attention to prayer. Make it the business of life. Be devoted to it. Just what he did himself, for Paul was a standing example of the doctrine of prayer which he advocated and pressed upon the people.

In his Epistles to the Thessalonians, how all-inclusive and wonderful the praying! Says he in writing his First Epistle to this Church:

"We give thanks to God always for you, making mention of you in my prayers; remembering without ceasing your work of faith, and labor of love, and patience of hope."

Not to quote all he says, it is worth while to read his words to this same Church of true believers further on:

"Night and day praying exceedingly that we might see your face, and might perfect that which is lacking in your faith. Now God himself direct our way unto you. And the Lord make you to increase and abound in love one toward another, even as we do toward you, to the end he may establish your hearts unblameable in holiness before God, even our Father."

And this sort of praying for these Thessalonian Christians is in direct line with that closing prayer for these same believers in this Epistle, where he records that striking prayer for their entire sanctification:

"And the very God of peace sanctify you wholly; and I pray God your whole spirit, and soul and body be preserved blameless unto the coming of our Lord Jesus Christ."

How Paul did pray for those early Christians! They were in his mind and on his heart, and he was continually at it, "night and day praying exceedingly." Oh, if we had a legion of preachers in these days of superficial piety and these times of prayerlessness, who were given to praying for their churches as Paul did for those to whom he ministered in his day! Praying men

Application to My Life:

are needed. Likewise praying preachers are demanded in this age.

At the conclusion of that remarkable prayer in the third chapter of Ephesians, he declared that "God was able to do exceeding abundantly above all that we could ask or think," now he declares he is praying exceeding abundantly, striving after the most earnest order, to have his prayers run parallel with God's power, and that they may not limit that power nor exhaust that power, but get all there is in it to bless and greatly enrich His Church.

Paul and his compeers prayed for the saints everywhere. It may be referred to again. With what solemnity does Paul call the attention of the Roman Christians to the important fact of praying for them, believers whom he had never seen! "God is my witness that without ceasing, I make mention of you in my prayers." To the churches he says, "Praying always for you."

Again on the same line, we hear him articulating dearly, "Always in every prayer of mine for you all, making request with joy." Again he writes thus: "I do not cease to pray for you." Once more we read the record, "Wherefore we pray always for you." And again it is written, "Cease not to give thanks for you, making mention of you in my prayers." And then he says, "Remembrance of thee in my prayers night and day."

His declaration, "night and day praying exceedingly," is a condensed record of the engrossing nature of the praying done by this praying apostle. It shows conclusively how important prayer was in his estimate and in his ministry, and further shows how to him prayer was an agony of earnest striving in seeking from God blessings which could be secured in no other way.

The unselfishness of his praying is seen in his writing to the Romans where he tells them, "Making request if by any means I might have a prosperous journey to come to you. For I long to see you that I may impart to you some spiritual gift to the end ye may be established." The object of his desire to visit Rome was not for selfish gratification, the pleasure of a trip, or for other reasons, but that he might be the means under God of "imparting to them some spiritual gift," in order that they "might be established" in their hearts, unblameably in love. It was that his visit might give to them some spiritual gift which they had not received and that they might be established at those points where they needed to be rooted, and grounded in faith, in love, and in all that made up Christian life and character.

Application to My Life:

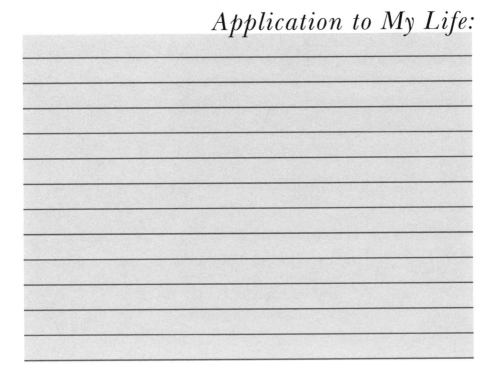

Chapter 15

Paul and His Requests
for Prayer

I desire above all things to learn to pray. We want to sound the reveille for the Christian warriors. We desire to find truth of the lack of real praying. What is it? Why is it? Why so little time spent in prayer when Christ, who had command of His time, chose to spend great part of it in INTERCESSION? "He ever liveth to make intercession for us." We believe the answer to be the desire is in the heart, but the will is undisciplined, the motive is present, but the affections have not melted under hours of heavenly meditation; the intellect is keen, yet not for hours of tireless research. The intellect and the affections have never been linked together by the sealing of the blessed Holy Ghost to do or die for God's glory in the secret places, with doors shut, lusts crucified.

—Rev. Homer W. Hodge

The many requests of Paul for prayer for himself, made to those to whom he ministered, put prayer to the front in Paul's estimate of its possibilities. Paul prayed much himself, and tried hard to arouse Christians to the imperative importance of the work of prayer. He so deeply felt the need of prayer that he was given to the habit of personal praying. Realizing this for himself, he pressed this invaluable duty upon others. Intercessory prayer, or prayer for others, occupied a high place in his estimate of prayer. It is no surprise, therefore, when we find him throwing himself upon the prayers of the churches to whom he wrote.

By all their devotion to Jesus Christ, by all their interest in the advance of God's kingdom on earth, by all the ardor of their personal attachment to Jesus, he charges them to pray much, to pray unceasingly, to pray at all times, to pray in all things, and to make praying a business of praying. And then

Application to My Life:

realizing his own dependence upon prayer for his arduous duties, his sore trials and his heavy responsibilities, he urges those to whom he wrote to pray especially for him.

The chief of the Apostles needed prayer. He needed the prayers of others, for this he practically admitted in asking for their prayers. His call to the apostleship did not lift him above this need. He realized and acknowledged his dependence on prayer. He craved and prized the prayers of all good people. He was not ashamed to solicit prayers for himself nor to urge the brethren everywhere to pray for him.

In writing to the Hebrews, he bases his request for prayer on two reasons, his honesty and his anxiety to visit them. If he were insincere, he could lay no claim to their prayers. Praying for him, it would be a powerful agent in facilitating his visit to them. They would touch the secret place of the wind and the waves, and arrange all secondary agencies and make them minister to this end. Praying puts God in haste to do for us the things which we wish at His hands.

Paul's frequent request of his brethren was that they would "pray for him." We are to judge of the value of a thing by the frequency of asking for it, and by the special and urgent plea made for it. If that be true, then with Paul the prayers of the saints were among his greatest assets. By the urgency, iteration and reiteration of the request, "Pray for me," Paul showed conclusively the great value he put upon prayer as a means of grace. Paul had no need so pressing as the need of prayer. There were no values so appreciated and appreciable as the prayers of the faithful.

Paul put the great factor of prayer as the great factor in his work. The most powerful and far-reaching energy in Paul's estimate is prayer. He covets it and hoards it as he seeks the prayers of God's people. The earnestness of his soul goes out in these requests. Hear him in this entreaty for prayer he is writing to the Romans:

> *"I beseech you, brethren, for the Lord Jesus Christ's sake, and for the love of the Spirit, that ye strive together with me in your prayers for me."*

Prayers by others for Paul were valuable because they helped him. Great helpers are prayers. Nothing gives so much aid to us in our needs as real prayers. They supply needs and deliver from straits. Paul's faith, so he writes to the Corinthians, had been much tried, and he had been much helped and much strengthened by God's deliverance. "Ye also helping by prayer." What marvelous things has God done for His favored saints through the prayers of others! The saints can help the saints more by fervent praying than in any other way.

Application to My Life:

In the midst of envy and detraction, and in perils by false brethren, he writes thus to the Philippians:

"For I know that this shall turn to my salvation though your prayer, and the supply of the Spirit of Jesus Christ.

"According to my expectation, and my hope, that in nothing I shall be ashamed, but with all boldness as always, so now also Christ shall be magnified in my body, whether it be by life or death."

Shame was taken away, holy boldness secured, and life and death made glorious by the prayers of the saints at Philippi for Paul.

Paul had many mighty forces in his ministry. His remarkable conversion was a great force, a point of mighty projecting and propelling power, and yet he did not in his ministry secure its results by the force of his epochal conversion. His call to the apostleship was clear, luminous, and all-convincing, but he did not depend on that for the largest results in his ministry.

Paul's course was more clearly marked out and his career rendered more powerfully successful by prayer than by any other force.

Paul urges the Roman Christians to pray for him that he may be delivered from unbelieving men. Prayer is a defense and protection against the malignity and machinations of evil men. It can affect men because God can affect them. Paul had not only unbelieving enemies with whom to contend, but many Christians were prejudiced against him to an extent which rendered it questionable whether they would accept any Christian service at his hands. Especially was this the case at Jerusalem, and so prayer, powerful prayer, must be used to remove the mighty and pernicious force of prejudice, inflamed and deep-seated.

Prayer on their part for him must be used for his safety, and also that a prosperous journey and God's will might bring him speedily and surely to them, in order to bless and refresh mutually the Roman Christians.

These prayer requests of Paul are many-sided and all-comprehensive. How many things does his request to the Roman Church include! The request for their prayers, like the Church to whom it is directed, is cosmopolitan. He beseeches them, entreats them, a term indicating intensity and earnestness, "for the sake of Jesus Christ, to strive with him in their prayers for him." This he desires that he may be delivered from evil and designing men, who might hinder and embarrass him in his mission, then further that his service for the poor saints

Application to My Life:

might be accepted by the saints, and that he might ultimately come unto them with joy that they might be refreshed.

How full of heart earnestness is his request! How tender and loving is his appeal! How touching and high is the motive to the highest and truest form of prayer, "for the Lord Jesus Christ's sake!" Also for the love we bear to the Spirit, or for the love which the Spirit bears to us; by the ties of the holy brotherhood. By these lofty and constraining motives does he urge them to pray for him and to "strive with him" in their mutual praying. Paul is in the great prayer struggle, a struggle in which the mightiest issues are involved and imperiled; and he is in the midst of this struggle. He is committed to it because Christ is in it. He needs help, help which comes alone through prayer. So he pleads with his brethren to pray for him and with him.

By prayer enemies are to be swept out of the way. By prayer prejudices are to be driven out of the hearts of good men. His way to Jerusalem would be cleared of difficulties, the success of his mission would be secured, and the will of God and the good of the saints would be accomplished. All these marvelous ends would be secured by marvelous praying. Wonderful and world-wide are the results to be gained by mighty praying. If all apostolic successors had prayed as Paul did, if all Christians in all these ages had been one with apostolical men in the mighty wrestlings of prayer, how marvelous and divine would have been the history of God's Church! How unparalleled would have been its success! The glory of its millennium would have brightened and blessed the world ages ago.

We see in Paul's requests his estimate of the far-reaching power of prayer. Not that prayer has in it any talismanic force, nor that it is a fetish, but that it moves God to do things that it nominates. Prayer has no magic, potent charm in itself, but is only all potent because it gets the Omnipotent God to grant its request. A precedent basis in all prayer as expressed or understood by Paul is that "Ye strive together with me in your prayers for me." It is of the nature of a severe conflict in which Paul's soul is engaged, a wrestle, a hand-to-hand fight. The strain is severe and exhaustive to all the energies of the soul, and the issue is tossed in uncertainty. Paul in this prayer struggle needs reinforcements and divine help in his striving. He is in the midst of the struggle, and will bear the brunt, but he solicits and pleads for the help of others. Their prayers are just now needed, He needs help to offer intense prayers.

Prayer is not inaptly called "wrestling," because it is a most intense struggle. To prayer there are the greatest hindrances and the most inveterate foes. Mighty evil forces surge around the closets of prayer. Enemies strong and strongly entrenched are about the closets where praying is done. No feeble, listless act is this praying done by Paul. In this thing he has

Application to My Life:

"put away childish things." The commonplace and the tame have been retired. Paul must do this praying mightily or not do it at all. Hell must feel and stagger and under the mightiness of his prayer stroke, or he strikes not at all. The strongest graces and the manliest efforts are requisite here. Strength is demanded in the praying done by Paul. Courage is at a premium in it. Timid touches and faint-hearted desires avail nothing in the mind of Paul which we are considering. Enemies are to be faced and routed and fields are to be won. The most unflagging and invincible bravery and the highest qualities of Christian soldierhood are demanded for prayer. It is a trumpet call to prayer, a chieftain's clarion note, sounded out for earnest, persistent prayer as the great spiritual conflict rages.

Chapter 16

Paul and His Requests For Prayer (Continued)

We announce the law of prayer as follows: A Christian's prayer is a joint agreement of the will and his cabinet, the emotions, the conscience, the intellect, working in harmony at white heat, while the body co-operates under certain hygienic conditions to make the prayer long enough sustained at high voltage to insure tremendous results, supernatural and unearthly.

—*Rev. Homer W. Hodge*

We come to the request of Paul made to the Church at Ephesus, found in the latter part of Ephes. 6 of the Epistle to those Christians:

"Praying always with all prayer and supplication in the Spirit, and watching thereunto with all perseverance and supplication for all saints;

"And for me that utterance may be given unto me, that I may open my mouth boldly, to make known the mystery of the Gospel,

"For which I am an ambassador in bonds, that therein I may speak boldly as I ought to speak."

For this Church he had labored and prayed night and day, with many watchings and tears and much humility. As he drew a vivid picture of the Christian soldier, with his foes

Application to My Life:

besetting him, he gave them this charge of praying specially for him.

To these Ephesian Christians he gave a comprehensive statement of the necessity, nature and special benefits of prayer. It was to be urgent, covering all times and embracing all manner of places. Supplication must give intensity, the Holy Spirit must be invoked, vigilance and perseverance must be added, and the whole family of saints were involved.

The force of his request for prayer centered on him, that he might be able to talk with force, fluency, directness and courage. Paul did not depend upon his natural gifts, but on those which came to him in answer to prayer. He was afraid he would be a coward, a dull, dry speaker, or a hesitating stammerer, and he urged these believers to pray that he might have courage, not only to speak clearly, but freely and fully.

He desired them to pray that he might have boldness. No quality seems more important to the preacher than that of boldness. It is that positive quality which does not reckon consequences, but with freedom and fullness meets the crisis, faces a present danger, and discharges unawed a present duty. It was one of the marked characteristics of apostolic preachers and apostolic preaching. They were bold men, they were bold preachers. The reference to the manifestation of the principle by them is almost the record of their trials. It is the applause of their faith.

There are many chains which enslave the preacher. His very tenderness makes him weak. His attachments to the people tend to bring him into bondage. His personal intercourse, his obligations to his people, his love for them, all tend to hamper his freedom and restrain his pulpit deliverances. What great need to be continually praying for boldness to speak boldly as he ought to speak!

The prophets of old were charged not to be afraid of the faces of men. Unawed by the frowns of men, they were to declare the truth of God without apology, timidity, hesitancy or compromise. The warmth and freedom of conviction and of sincerity, the fearlessness of a vigorous faith, and above all the power of the Holy Ghost, are all wonderful helpers and elements of boldness. How all this should be coveted and sought with all earnestness by ministers of the Gospel in this day!

Meekness and humility are high virtues of the first importance in the preacher, but these qualities do not at all militate against boldness. This boldness is not the freedom of passionate utterances. It is not scolding nor rashness. It speaks the truth in love. Boldness is not rudeness. Roughness

Application to My Life:

dishonors boldness. It is as gentle as a mother with a babe, but as fearless as a lion standing before a foe. Fear, in the mild and innocent form of timidity, or in the criminal form of cowardice, has no place in the true ministry. Humble but holy boldness is of the very first importance.

What hidden, mysterious mighty force can add courage to apostolical preaching, and give bolder utterances to apostolic lips? There is one answer, and it is that prayer can do the deed.

What force can so affect and dominate evil that the very results of evil will be changed into good? We have the answer in Paul's words again, in connection with prayers made for him:

"Who delivered us from so great a death, and doth deliver; in whom we trust that he will yet deliver us; Ye also helping together in prayer for us. What then? Notwithstanding every way, whether in pretense or in truth, Christ is preached, and therein I do rejoice, yea, and will rejoice."

We can see how the promises of God are made real and personal by prayer. "All things work together for good to them that love God." Here is a jeweled promise. Paul loved God, but he did not leave the promise alone, as a matter of course, to work out its blessed results. So he wrote to the Corinthians as we have before seen, "I am in trouble. I trust in God to deliver. Ye also helping together by prayer." Helping me by prayer, you help God to make the promise strong and rich in realization.

Paul's prayer requests embraced "supplication for all saints," but especially for apostolic courage for himself. How much he needed this courage just as all true preachers, called of God, need it! Prayer was to open doors for apostolical labors, but at the same time it was to open apostolic lips to utter bravely and truly the apostolic message.

Hear him as he speaks to the Church at Colosses:

"Withal praying also for us, that God would open to us a door of utterance to speak the mystery of Christ, for which I am also in bonds;

"That I may make it manifest as I ought to speak."

How appropriate such a request to be made by a present-day preacher to his congregation! How great the need of those things by the present-day preacher which Paul desired for himself!

As in the request to the Ephesians, Paul wants a "door of utterance" given him, that he may preach with the liberty of the Spirit, be delivered from being straitened in thought or hampered in delivery. Furthermore, he desires the ability to make manifest in the clearest terms, without confusion of thought,

Application to My Life:

and with force of utterance, the Gospel "as he ought to speak," and just as every preacher should speak. Happy that preacher who ministers to a people who pray thus for him!

And happier still if he inwardly feels, as he faces his responsible task and realizes how much he needs these things to preach clearly, forcibly and effectively, that he has urged his people to pray for him!

Prayer transmutes crosses, trials and oppositions into blessings, and causes them to work together for good. "These shall turn to my salvation through your prayers," says Paul. Just as the same things today in the life of the preacher are transmuted into gracious blessings in the end, "ye also helping together by prayer." Saintly praying mightily helped Apostolic preaching and rescued apostolic men from many sore straits. So just such praying in these days will effect like results in faithful preaching done by brave, fearless ministers. Prayer for the preacher avails just as prayer by the preacher avails. Two things are always factors in the life and work of a true preacher: First when he prays constantly, fervently and persistently for those to whom he preaches; and secondly, when those to whom he ministers pray for their preacher. Happy is the preacher so situated. Blessed is that congregation thus favored.

To the Church at Thessalonica Paul sends this pressing request, pointed, clear, and forcible:

"Finally, brethren, pray for us, that the word of the Lord may have free course, and be glorified, even as it is with you;

"And that we may be delivered from wicked and unreasonable men."

He has in mind a race-course, on which the racer is exerting himself to reach the goal. Hindrances are in the way of his success and must be removed, so that the racer may finally succeed and obtain the reward. The "Word of the Lord" is this racer, as preached by Paul. This Word is personified and there are serious impediments which embarrass the running of the Word. It must have "free course." Everything in the way and opposing its running must be taken out of its roadway. These impediments in the way of the Word of the Lord "running and being glorified" are found in the preacher himself, in the Church to whom he ministers, and in the sinners around him. The Word runs and is glorified when it has unobstructed access to the minds and hearts of those to whom it is preached, when sinners are convicted for sin, when they seriously consider the claims of God's Word on them, and when they are induced to pray for themselves, asking for pardoning mercy. It is glorified when saints are instructed in religious experience, corrected of errors of doctrine and mistakes in practice, and when they are

Application to My Life:

led to seek for higher things and to pray for deeper experiences in the Divine life.

Mark you. It is not when the preacher is glorified because of the wonderful success wrought by the Word. It is not when people praise him unduly, and make much of him because of his wonderful sermons, his great eloquence and his remarkable gifts. The preacher is kept in the background in all this work of glorification, even though he is foremost as being the object of all this praying.

Prayer is to do all these things. So Paul urges, entreats, insists, "Pray for us." And it is not so much prayer for Paul personally in his Christian life and religious experience. All this needed much prayer. It was really for him officially, prayer for him in the office and work of a Gospel minister. His tongue must be unloosed in preaching, his mouth unstopped, and his mind set free. Prayer must help in his religious life not so much because it would help to "work out his own salvation," but rather because right living would give strength to the Word of the Lord, and would save him from being a hindrance to the Word which he preached. And as he desires that no hindrance should be in himself which would defeat his own preaching, so he wants all hindrances taken away from the churches to whom he ministers that Church people may not stand in the way or weigh down the Word as it runs on the race-course attempting to reach the goal, even the minds and hearts of the people. Furthermore, he wishes hindrances in the unsaved to be set aside that God's Word as preached by him may reach their hearts and be glorified in their salvation.

With all this before him, Paul sends this pressing request to these believers at Thessalonica, "Pray for us," because praying by true Christians would greatly help in the running of the Word of the Lord.

Wise that preacher who has the eyes to see these things, and who realizes that his success largely depends upon praying of this kind on the part of his people for him. How much do we need churches now who, having the preacher in mind and the preached Word on their hearts, pray for him that "the Word of the Lord may have free course, and be glorified."

One other item in this request is worth noting: "That we may be delivered from wicked and unreasonable men." Such men are hindrances in the way of the Word of the Lord. Few preachers but are harassed by them and need to be delivered from them. Prayer helps to bring such a deliverance to preachers from "unreasonable and wicked men." Paul was annoyed by such characters, and for this very reason he urged prayer for him that he might find deliverance from them.

Application to My Life:

Summing it all up, we find that Paul feels that the success of the Word, its liberty and largeness, are bound up in their prayers, and that their failure to pray would restrict its influence and its glory. His deliverance from unreasonable and wicked men as well as his safety, he asserts, are in some way dependent upon their prayers. These prayers, while they greatly helped him to preach, would at the same time protect his person from the cruel purposes of wicked and unreasonable men.

In Hebrews 13:9, Paul thus opens his heart to those Hebrew Christians in asking them to pray for him:

"Pray for us, for we trust we have a good conscience, in all things willing to live honestly."

In this prayer request, Paul's inward consciousness of his integrity of heart and his internal witness to his personal honesty come out and are a basic truth of his Christian character. No room for blame does he find in himself. "Pray for us." Your prayers for us will find in me honest integrity and honest execution and honest administration of all prayer results.

The request is intended to stir up the saints to more earnest praying, more devotion to prayer, and more urgency in prayer. Prayer must affect his visit to them, would hasten it and enlarge its beneficial results.

Paul is on the most cordial and freest terms with Philemon. He is anxious and expects to visit him at some future day and makes the appointment. He takes it for granted that Philemon is praying, for as this man had been converted under his ministry, it is assumed that he has been taught the Pauline lesson of prayer. He assumes also that prayer will open up the way for his visit, remove the hindrances and bring them graciously together. So he requests Philemon to prepare a lodging place for him, adding, "I trust through your prayers I shall be given to you." Paul had the idea that his movements were hindered or helped by the prayers of his brethren.

Application to My Life: